How People with Autism Grieve, and How to Help

How People with Autism Grieve, and How to Help

AN INSIDER HANDBOOK

Deborah Lipsky

Jessica Kingsley *Publishers*
London and Philadelphia

First published in 2013
by Jessica Kingsley Publishers
116 Pentonville Road
London N1 9JB, UK
and
400 Market Street, Suite 400
Philadelphia, PA 19106, USA

www.jkp.com

Library of Congress Cataloging in Publication Data
Lipsky, Deborah.
  How people with autism grieve, and how to help : an insider handbook /
Deborah Lipsky.
    pages cm
  ISBN 978-1-84905-954-1 (alk. paper)
  1. Autistic people--Psychology. 2. Autism--Psychological aspects. 3. Loss
(Psychology) 4. Grief. I. Title.
  RC553.A88L568 2013
  616.85'882--dc23
                                2013008474

British Library Cataloguing in Publication Data
A CIP catalogue record for this book is available from the British Library

ISBN 978 1 84905 954 1
eISBN 978 0 85700 789 6

Printed and bound in Great Britain by Bell & Bain Ltd, Glasgow

Contents

How This Book Came About

I decided to write a book on understanding grief and loss because the death of my closest friend in 2010 truly pointed out significant differences on how people with autism grieve compared to non-autistic people. The expectations of the non-autistic world revolving around death and dying collide with the autistic perceptions of death and dying. Autistic individuals like me tend to become solitary creatures when faced with overwhelming stressful situations. We seek refuge alone in our own safe little world of a special interest or pursuit. We fiercely hang on to our rituals and routines. This sharply conflicts with the non-autistic world seeking solidarity in sharing their painful situations and grief with others, especially surrounding death.

The ending of any meaningful relationship, whether it is from death, divorce, or geographical separation, creates a grief response. The most common question

I get asked while conducting seminars on autism is, "Do autistic people cry?" There is this misperception out there that autistic individuals lack empathy and are disconnected from their emotions. This is only reinforced by the outward observance of some of our "unconventional" behaviors during such a stressful event. Nothing could be further from the truth. Our grieving process is different; not non-existent. We don't adhere to the universally accepted five stages of grief that western society has embraced. We do cry and we do feel the pain of loss. It is my hope that this book will help you understand how we grieve and tend to deal with any significant loss. I will provide you with strategies that will help you help us during such times. This is not a psychology textbook on human emotion. It is an honest firsthand account of how we autistics process the grief associated with the loss of someone in our life.

Discussing death and dying is such a morbid topic that its sheer unpleasantness tends to have us avoiding the subject until a loss occurs. My concern is for all of us autistic adults with aging parents who will have to face this stark reality some day. The death of my mother is unthinkable. The death of my husband, who is 18 years older than me, is a reality I am reluctant to face. There are autistic children deeply attached to an aging grandparent. Questions need to be answered. How will we handle such loss? How can you help us during such a time? Death brings about dramatic change and people with autism do not embrace change with open arms. How do you break the news that someone we are close to has died? Do you modify or completely change an autistic routine that involved the person who has died? What about our participation in the wake, funeral, or memorial service? Why are we behaving in such an inappropriate and selfish manner?

In 2010 my colleague, mentor, and dear friend Will Richards died from leukemia. We had been very close for the previous five years and my weekly visits with established routines were mutually anticipated and enjoyed by us both. His diagnosis came as a shock, and shortly thereafter our routine was suddenly and abruptly thrown into chaos as he underwent chemotherapy and lengthy hospital stays. My weekly time with him used to be a one on one relationship without other people to distract us. Being autistic I have difficulty relating to more than one person at a time unless I am the one in charge of the conversation, such as when I am the speaker at a presentation.

All of a sudden our afternoons together became isolated short visits based on daily conditions which were always in fluctuation. Unpredictability was the new norm and I had great difficulty trying to adhere to continuous change. Friends and family invaded the time I spent with him, turning our one on one relationship into group gatherings. I could not adapt to that because in my autistic way of thinking, I was friends with Will only, not all his relatives and well-wishers. I became increasingly frustrated by what I saw as an "invasion" into our time together and a total dismantling of the immoveable structure of a five-year routine. I had no interest listening to three or four way conversations about things other than what Will and I used to talk about. To complicate matters even more, as the room filled with other well-wishers, the sheer "crowd" caused my autistic mannerisms to become painfully obvious. Although most of his visitors knew I had autism, many of them were unprepared to see a 48-year-old woman displaying such behaviors as rocking and hand stimming which only intensified as my anxiety level kept creeping higher due to a constant stream of people entering and leaving his room.

No one wanted to talk about the inevitable fact that he could die. There was great hope in remissions and state of the art treatments. Conversations always focused on everything but the disease at hand. I remember sitting and listening to the conversations of others. Sports, the weather, or other such trivial matters were the dominant theme. Will used to always reassure me that he would beat this disease and not "abandon" me (I have some real abandonment issues that I am trying to overcome). Our routine would resume once he was better. I trusted him whole-heartedly. I know now he said those things out of love, trying to prevent unnecessary worry over a very uncertain future. At the time however, as he got sicker I became angry that he was lying to me about how things will get better some day. I needed the brutal truth and that was something no one wanted to address. I needed a script to deal with the aftermath of his death, but I found no template in the traditional books on grieving. I needed people not to judge me because of how I came to grips with his death, but there was no autistic book written on the subject that I could hand to them.

I never went to the memorial service or even visited him in the hospital as he got close to dying. I never kept in contact with his family thereafter. I threw away all photos and mementos of our friendship; I had no need for sentimentality. I didn't even mention his name after he died. I never reminisced about the good times we had together. What was the use? I always felt that indulging in past memories was a powerful narcotic that could be addicting. Will was gone out of my life forever and the only sensible thing to do was to move forward without looking back. To those around me, this attitude was viewed as callous, insensitive, and just plain wrong.

It has taken over two years for me to come to understand how my grieving differed from those around Will. It's not that I had no feelings towards losing him. On the contrary, I had such intense feelings that they overwhelmed me. This created a continued state of anxiety made worse by the societal expectations surrounding a dying loved one. The lessons and insights I have learned from this experience are contained in this book. I have talked with other autistic individuals who have experienced a death, and I found that their coping mechanisms that enabled them to come to grips with this reality mirrored mine. May this book enlighten you as to how we handle grief, and may this book create a deeper empathy and compassion towards an autistic person experiencing such a devastating loss.

CHAPTER 1

Differences in Dealing with Problems

Before launching straight away into the grieving process, it is imperative that you understand that there is a vast difference in how we autistics deal with stress, problems, and grief. Please understand that autism covers a wide spectrum and we are all individuals. There is no one book on autism that can be applied 100 percent to every person with autism. This book will offer you an insight into how and why many autistics handle and process grief in our own unique and nonconformist way. It isn't designed to be a one-size-fits-all approach that can be applied to every autistic person out there. Where the person is on the autism spectrum is an important factor in determining how well they can process a traumatic event. This book will provide general guidelines on how you can not only understand how we process grief but also better help us in the grieving process.

How we as human beings approach death, dying, and grief is shaped by familial and cultural expectations. In all honesty, much of processing the death experience is a learned response. We (society) are taught that the participation in wakes and funerals helps with closure. Certain customs are observed. We are reminded that during the grieving process it is "expected" to want to comfort someone who is mourning. A well-intended phrase such as "Sorry for your loss" seems obligatory when confronting a mourner.

In both my seminars and consultation business, the two most frequently asked questions I receive revolves around our apparent "insensitivity" to others' feelings, particularly when it comes to our reaction or lack of it to another person's negative emotion such as sadness. "Why is it that autistic people seem so indifferent towards our emotional needs and are unable to offer support or at least empathy during such a traumatic event?" "Do autistic people cry?"

Yes, we do cry and our "indifference" isn't intentional; it's part of our autistic mindset.

The major differences in how we approach a difficult situation

THE NON-AUTISTIC APPROACH TO DEALING WITH GRIEF

The way an autistic person approaches the same problem a non-autistic person does is totally opposite. People without autism tend to have a deeper connection to processing how they are feeling when faced with an overwhelming stressor. When shocking news hits a non-autistic person, their immediate reaction is to want not only to tell someone else but also to "share" how they are feeling about that situation. People tend to look for solidarity such as gathering at candlelight vigils to honor a recently slain person or people, joining support groups where they can connect with others in similar emotional states, or just be with friends and family during their time of emotional distress. Some may become advocates to help others in similar tragedies which also aids in their emotional healing. For a small percentage who are unable to deal with their emotions, they will turn to self-medication, be it alcohol, drugs, or some other self-destructive behaviors.

When faced with a crisis many will tend to want to express how they feel to someone who helps them not "feel" so alone during that time. During the uncertainty of moment or crisis, many non-autistic individuals find security in having someone there for them. Receiving hugs of consolation seems to offer comfort as does someone just staying with that person as moral support. In general it is this innate need to share their emotions with someone else, as well as an innate need to be there by those close to that person to offer support for a grieving individual. Acknowledgment by another to an individual experiencing a loss allows the grieving person in a small way not to feel alone. By telling someone else, the tragedy becomes a reality as the certainty of the situation can now no longer be denied.

Of course this doesn't apply to every non-autistic person. Environmental factors, culture, and family upbringing shape how people learn to respond to tragic events in their life. How children are indoctrinated in the home to the whole process of comforting and nurturing will greatly determine their response as adults. The way children tend to model the grieving process is shaped by the actions and behaviors of their parents or those in charge of their care. The number of deaths within a family also plays a determining factor in shaping a child's perception of death. Our western society expects a certain amount of sympathy and empathy to be shown to those undergoing a tragic loss. Societal and cultural etiquette surrounding death is largely comprised of unwritten rules that when not followed make the person out to be a callous cold-hearted individual. There is great variance in those unwritten rules. For example, how long should a widow or widower wait before re-entering the dating world? These rules are subjective, not concrete, and are based on many external factors as well as the mindset of non-autistic people. It is, however, still the mainstream approach by the non-autistic society to be concerned foremost with the emotional impacts of tragedy and loss.

Let's look at when someone dies. The wake, funeral service, or memorial service are opportunities for family members and friends to comfort and console mourners. It is a natural inclination to be with the grieving person just to offer emotional support. There is an apparent need for consoling hugs and offering words of encouragement of some sort. For many people it is a time when they do not want to be alone and truly appreciate having someone else around to share their grief. Cultural values expect those in the funeral party to act and behave in a certain way to show respect to the deceased person as well as to the mourners. The "comforters" may be inclined to go out of their way and routine to help with the needs of those who are grieving, be it physical or emotional. They will offer to listen any time the mourner just needs to talk. It is an act of great selflessness towards the grieving individual. The main focus initially tends to be on the emotional well-being of the mourner. Friends and relatives may assist in making arrangements and preparations for the funeral to allow the mourner to just "grieve" their loss leading up to the funeral. This eliminates the burden of having to perform daily chores during that time.

SEPTEMBER 11, 2001 AND OTHER NATIONAL TRAGEDIES

I remember that terrible day on September 11, 2001 when the World Trade Center towers were hit by hijacked planes. The television was a nonstop news feed of reactions of shock, anxiety, and utter disbelief. I received many phone calls from people I knew that weren't even close friends asking me if I had heard what happened and what my response was. All over the United States people were crying in each other's arms, many unable to function as they tried to process emotionally what had just occurred. Emotionally charged displays of patriotism were evident in just about every neighborhood in the United States. Initially churches were full to capacity in the World Trade Center aftermath. People sought emotional comfort and felt compelled to do something even if it was just to pray or hold candlelight vigils for those killed in the attack. For a time afterwards in every public place the main focus and topic of discussion was on the terrorist attack. People needed to "vent" their feelings of frustration, anger, and anxiety to others. Somehow sharing those feelings with another person brought relief and a sense of solidarity. The emotion of patriotism was very pronounced. Emotions ran high.

Anger and rage with a collective need for vengeance also surfaced. The emotion of fear, whether founded or unfounded, dominated many people's thoughts. Incidences of hate crimes targeting Muslim American citizens began to surface. People of Middle Eastern descent who had no connection to the terrorists of 9/11 or to any anti-American group were at risk of being targeted by other individuals based solely on the color of their skin, how they dressed, or what religion they practiced. This targeting at that time was based solely on emotions and not on facts. This wasn't an isolated incident.

History proves time and time again that society tends to react and behave emotionally immediately following a national tragedy before actually thinking through the logical aspects of their desires and actions. When the Japanese Navy bombed Pearl Harbor, the United States government rounded up all Japanese-American US citizens and sent them to internment camps in the desert for the duration of the war. Deportation to these camps wasn't based on evidence of anti-American activity but based solely on their nationality. If you looked oriental, you were held in suspicion by most Americans at the time. As an autistic person it baffles me as to why society tends to gravitate towards processing and expressing their emotional feelings ahead of logical and factual problem-solving interventions.

For the non-autistic person, what is important is getting in touch with their feelings, particularly grief and letting them out. There is a need to reach out for comfort and to be reassured by another human being. During a tragedy there is a need to be with others to discuss how the event impacts them emotionally. Cases of post-traumatic stress disorder rose sharply in the

American population following 9/11, as many people became fearful of future attacks as their inner sense of invincibility was shattered that day.

Traveling became a nightmare as homeland security enacted many strict traveling procedures to protect its travelers in the 9/11 aftermath. While I totally agree that this was warranted, some guidelines were illogical. I struggled with why my cosmetic metal nail file was confiscated while flying to a speaking engagement. I was told it was banned as it was considered a weapon. I don't remember the terrorists using a cosmetic case as their arsenal bag when they hijacked the planes. Any object that could be constructed into a weapon has now been banned, but from a rational standpoint that is illogical. A nail file could be used to stab someone but so could a pen or pencil, yet they are allowed on the plane. Still such measures give the average non-autistic person a sense of security, a good feeling that something is being done by the authorities to prevent another such attack. From the autistic vantage point, much of it seems to have been thought through emotionally rather than logically.

It is generally the non-autistic approach to react emotionally to a tragedy. When something really tragic occurs, emotions can cloud reason. This is how wars begin, and vigilante mobs take the law into their own hands. I am not trying to berate non-autistic people, but take an honest look at how history proves this true. Hitler with his overly emotionally frenzied rhetoric rallied an entire nation by playing on their emotions to take part in one of the worst atrocities of the twentieth century. Mob mentality is fueled not by logic but by powerful emotionally charged rhetoric. Just look at the growing conflicts in the Middle East. One act of violence seems to mobilize protesters who rally in the streets crying out for revenge. Non-autistic people tend to first look at problems and loss from an emotional point of view; how the loss will impact their emotional well-being.

I don't want to sound callous but when I watched the news coverage of 9/11 on television, I was hit with a sense of shock and surprise too. My initial focus centered on the practicality of whether flying would ever be a viable option. I immediately began to process screening procedures and pondered how from a logical standpoint terrorists even made it on the plane. Because the tragedy didn't directly affect any of my routines, I felt no emotional connection to this event. I only watched about a half hour of news coverage to gain the facts and then I resumed my daily routines. I received numerous calls from neighbors, friends, and acquaintances that day wondering if I had heard what had happened. I became annoyed because they wanted to just talk about what they were feeling and that was interfering with my routines. This was a time when cell phones hadn't reached the popularity they have today and I was tethered to a telephone cord unable to go about engaging in my normal routines. I found the telephone calls much more distressing than the tragedy itself because I was prevented from engaging in my routines, which provided the sense of comfort I needed to deal with the uncertainty of our nation's traveling infrastructure at that moment. In the midst of such unpredictability, all I wanted was to maintain my sense of predictability by following one of my many daily rituals and routines. All my energy was being poured into that endeavor. I had no reserve available for dealing with other people's emotions. I immediately went out and bought an answering machine for my telephone that same day. This way I was able to screen calls and answer only those not dealing with 9/11.

Our autistic incessant need for maintaining predictability through rituals and routines dominates our every thought. Our emotions are directly tied to this. We seem to be so indifferent emotionally to what is happening around us as long as it doesn't directly affect us. That is partly due to the fact that we expend a lot of mental energy ensuring our own stability. Our brains are wired to focus more on the logical rather than on the emotional aspects of an event. The first question that dominates our thinking is, "How will this event affect me?" Our priority is to secure our sense of well-being ahead of anyone else's; otherwise we cannot function at all during a traumatic event.

"IT'S ALL ABOUT ME": THE AUTISTIC MINDSET

The autistic individual approaches problems from a completely different angle. Autistic people when confronted with a problem have a tendency to focus not on how they "feel" initially but on problem solving. We live in our own world dominated by our own scripts, rituals, and routines. Anything that takes us off our intended script causes acute anxiety. If I had to sum up our way of thinking in one phrase I would say, "It's all about me." For all you caregivers and professionals working with the autistic population, you know exactly what I am saying. It sounds selfish, but that is how our brains are wired. How many of you go to great lengths to ensure that your client, spouse, friend, or child maintains their routines so as to not create a meltdown response? We derive our inner sense of security from unchanging daily rituals and routines.

From the non-verbal right up the spectrum to high functioning autistic, we create our own environment where we are concerned with maintaining our own sense of security and routine. To fully understand this I strongly recommend that you read my book *From Anxiety to Meltdown* (published by Jessica Kingsley) to get a deeper understanding of how we process the world around us. For us, our day is just one script after another. Adhering to routines provides us with such a sense of inner calm and tranquility. To be brutally honest, for the average autistic individual, maintaining our little world of routines takes precedence over other people's feelings, intentions, needs, or expectations. Our focus regarding people around us tends to be on how they will conform to our routines. It sounds rather manipulative and in a sense it is, but it isn't done out of malice. Our unending need for predictability requires that you (who are part of our routine) assimilate into our concept of predictability within that routine.

"I DON'T CARE HOW I FEEL, FIX THE PROBLEM!"

A dramatic or sudden change in a routine will elicit quite an emotional outburst and deep sense of panic and anxiety in an autistic individual. I refer to them as "novel situations" where it is something unplanned out of the ordinary that will directly impact an autistic person's day. The highly charged emotional outburst is due to the fact that our sense of inner calm has been shattered by an unforeseen, unplanned circumstance disrupting that routine. We literally have this horrific sense of no control over our environment which is so distressing to us internally that it is unbearable. Many of you who have witnessed a meltdown response will know exactly what I mean. There will be wailing and gnashing of the teeth from an autistic child or adult over what may appear to others as something minor, such as driving to a planned activity like swimming only to find the public pool closed due to some malfunction of the pool filters. It isn't the loss of the activity as much as the disruption of going off script that caused the emotional outburst. It is the panic over losing a viable script and having nothing (no plan) to replace it.

It is the natural tendency of a non-autistic person to want to deal first with the emotional aspect of the situation by attempting to soothe and calm the autistic individual having an emotional outburst reaction to a novel situation. Reassuring phrases that things will work out in the end seem to fall on deaf ears. The more we are asked to calm down, the more we tend to escalate. It almost seems implausible, but in that heightened emotional state we are totally unaware of what we are feeling. The panic and fear are solely focused on the break in the continuity of a routine or script. Our mind desperately obsesses on restoring the natural order of our created routines and scripts. At that moment how we are feeling is so insignificant compared to finding a solution to the problem. We don't want to be told to calm down; we need to fix the problem. The only way to break through this is by offering logical solutions or options to the problem at hand initially, and then dealing with the emotional aspects of the meltdown afterwards.

It is not so much losing the activity as it is going off script that causes severe distress. I advocate always having a backup script or a plan that is communicated beforehand so that the autistic individual has a sense of structure. The phrase I recommend and also use on me starts out with, "In the unlikely event that…" For instance, "In the unlikely event that the public swimming pool is closed, we will then instead spend the hour playing miniature golf."

I use that phrase many times throughout my daily routines, whether it be going grocery shopping or mowing the lawn. I actually have a fleet of five lawn mowers as a backup plan because my routine of mowing the lawn every Friday is so important and integral to my inner sense of well-being, I can't risk that routine being broken by malfunctioning equipment.

So in general when it comes to handling problems, the autistic mindset is focused on problem solving; coming up with viable alternatives that restore our inner sense of well-being. Our emotional needs are irrelevant to us at the moment. During the crisis we are totally unaware of what impact our emotional state has on others. What we need most from you first is an action plan or script that can help restore predictability in our lives. Try to correct the problem at hand and have backup scripts at the ready to employ during a catastrophic reaction to an unplanned circumstance.

It is important to understand that usually when an autistic individual is faced with a significant stressor, our inclination is to seek isolation as opposed to comfort from someone else. Instead of wanting to "share" our problematic situation with another, we prefer to isolate away. For many of us we will hyper-focus and take consolation from engaging in our special interest. This is done for a few reasons. I will cover this in depth in Chapter 2.

Death: when there is no "fix" for the problem

NO BACKUP PLANS FOR THE DEATH OF A LOVED ONE

For most meltdowns and catastrophic reactions, the strategies I just outlined are very helpful. When it comes to the death of a loved one, however, there will be no immediate solution to the disruption of that autistic individual's routines. It will be very challenging for the caregiver, friend, or professional because there will be no way to "fix" the problem. I feel the only and best strategy to handle this difficult situation is to have a script and plan in place before and after a significant death occurs. This is a very difficult task because in our culture no one wants to address the mortality of their loved ones. The other option will be to create a brand new script to help ease the abrupt transition caused by an unexpected death. You must initially focus on restoring a sense of predictability by either restoring a routine or creating a very concrete replacement.

At the age of 51, I successfully obtained my motorcycle license and I now have two motorcycles I love to ride. While I am very safety orientated I also realize that there is an inherent risk of dying in a motorcycle crash that didn't exist before now. To be practical and from a logical standpoint, I have attempted to discuss what should be done in the unlikely event of my untimely demise with both my husband and my mother. Both of them became very upset and adamantly refused to talk about it with me, repeating over and over, "I just can't go there with you; you are not going to die." The mere thought of my death stirs up such deep feelings of despair, they choose to ignore the reality that

I will die one day whether they are prepared or not for it. Not talking about the reality of death won't make it go away; it will only serve to further enhance the feeling of loss when that time comes.

WELL-INTENDED BUT NOT HELPFUL

When Will, my closest friend and colleague, was diagnosed with leukemia, he initially kept reassuring me that he was going to beat this disease and not die. The odds for his survival were very unfavorable. Still he insisted that after his lengthy treatments in hospital were over, we would resume our usual visiting routine. He promised he wouldn't leave me. It has taken me years to understand that he said those things because he loved me and was trying to protect me from the pain he knew I would experience at his death. At the time, however, I became very angry. With his deteriorating physical condition, every hospital visit was unpredictable and at times chaotic. I kept pressuring him for a game plan or a script of what to do when he died. He didn't want to talk about it so we never did. There was a brief remission period where he and I were able to resume our usual weekly routine, followed by more reassurances from him that he wasn't going to die. The fact of the matter was that the remission didn't last long. His relapse was even more severe and pronounced, throwing me for a second time into such a chaotic world of unpredictability that I almost suffered a mental breakdown. The stress of not being able to cope with all the daily uncertainties, combined with no script for handling his eventual demise, left me totally ill-equipped to deal with his death.

I know it is a noble gesture to want to reassure loved ones that all will be well when the outcome looks bleak. Non-autistic people do this to spare those that they love undue grief and worry. It is truly an act of love to care more about how someone else is feeling and thereby hide the stark reality of death from them for the moment. The concern for someone's immediate emotional state overshadows the practical implications of dealing with the inevitable. It is well-intended but not practical for the autistic individual that will be impacted by that person's death.

In my seminars I always remind my attendees that people with autism hate surprises. We don't embrace radical change or spontaneity very graciously. The more notice we have that a change is coming, the better we are able to accommodate change in our affected routine. Ideally the best time to slowly acclimatize an autistic individual to the concept of a loved one dying is well in advance of their death. Please don't wait until that person is on their death bed to begin to discuss that death is imminent. With sudden death there is no planning; I will cover this topic later in the book.

As a child I was deeply attached to my grandfather. We had a special routine whenever I saw him and I loved him so much. His health began to falter over the course of a few years but that knowledge was kept from me. One day he had a stroke. My mother felt it best not to burden me with the gravity of the situation. She opted to tell me not to worry and that things would be OK. Things weren't OK and my grandfather died as a result of his stroke. I never saw his death coming and the shock was so severe that I fell into a deep despair that negatively affected my health at the time. I had no script or plan for handling the loss of a significant part of my life and routine.

The notion of him ever dying was never a reality because it was never discussed. Of course I am not faulting my mother for this. She doesn't have autism and from her standpoint she was only trying to protect me from undue emotional pain by withholding the facts of his failing health. There are many parents of autistic children today who can relate to their child with autism being emotionally attached to a grandparent, parent, sibling, relative, or close friend. Considering bringing up the topic of death when all is well and death isn't imminent doesn't seem like a viable option in dealing with transition planning. Death is, however, *the* transition that demands a plan of action in order to adequately cope with loss of security, predictability, and routine that accompanies losing a loved one.

Of course there is a fine line as to when is the appropriate time to discuss such a delicate topic. Factors such as where the individual is on the spectrum, what impact the loss will have on daily routines, when the loss will occur (such as in the case of terminal illness or geriatric considerations), and the relationship to the person with autism must be taken into account. Don't wait until a significant death occurs to begin to address the issue of death with an autistic person.

For the most part the initial focus from the autistic standpoint will be on the practical ramifications surrounding the death of someone significant in their life. Our tendency isn't to seek out the comfort of others, but to try to maintain or create a sense of normalcy through rituals, routines, and special interests. There will be a tendency to be preoccupied with him or herself as opposed to focusing on the needs of others directly affected by the loss. The crying and distress initially will be more centered on how the death of that person ruined their routine or daily structure. Although this may seem very callous and shallow, I assure you that isn't the case. We do feel intense emotional pain but our nature dictates that we deal with the practical consequences (as it affects us personally) before our brain can process the emotional aspects of the situation. I cannot stress this enough, but please focus on helping us find solutions to our broken routines caused by someone's death before focusing on only our emotional well-being. By coming up with practical strategies that deal with our physical existence, you will be contributing to the restoration of our emotional well-being.

CHAPTER 2

Emotional Expressions of Grief in Autism

I did an internet search on death and autism and I came across only a handful of articles on the subject. I read through most of these articles and found them redundant in their strategies, with virtually no focus on the emotional aspects from an autistic point of view. Erroneous conclusions were drawn on how we autistics grieve emotionally based on the non-autistic model of five stages of grieving by Elisabeth Kübler-Ross back in the 1960s. A further internet search about this grieving process model revealed numerous scientific studies done since that time period which disproves that model of grieving all together. Human resilience combined with spirituality plays a major role in how a person handles death, according to the other studies. Still, it is an established approach adopted by the mainstream populace today. As I reflected on this grieving model, I felt that the majority of autistic individuals out there would experience such a myriad of individual different reactions to grief that it would be hard to categorize them into stages.

In Chapter 1, I explained how autistic individuals when faced with a crisis have a foremost need to problem solve before even acknowledging their emotions. Since 2004 I have discussed the topic of emotional expression hundreds of times with fellow autistic individuals. While we vary greatly in this regard, there is a consensus among our population that there are commonalties inherent to our autistic nature revolving around emotional expression. It is a myth to assume that people with autism are incapable of emotional expression. Just look at how emotionally charged a meltdown or catastrophic reaction can be. In this chapter I will attempt to give you insights into our emotional processing during the grieving period and how it may appropriately or inappropriately manifest itself. The degree of emotional detachment will vary greatly from individual to individual. Where an individual is on the autism spectrum, combined with environmental factors, will influence emotional expression and awareness. For those individuals who received instruction in emotional regulation and expression, this too will affect the degree of awareness and expression. How an individual is exposed to the whole concept of death and dying greatly influences thoughts and behaviors.

Initial shock and disbelief upon hearing someone has died

I believe that for the most part that initial shock is a universal emotion whether someone is autistic or not. Granted, for a small percentage of people who are involved in long or terminal illness cases, shock may be absent as death seems like a merciful relief from the physical suffering. Under those conditions death brings a sense of relief and closure. I am focusing more on unexpected or sudden death scenarios, for example, receiving a call out of the blue that your sister died of a heart attack at age 50, or your son or daughter was killed in an automobile crash.

Initially there is this complete sense of disbelief that someone you know and are close to has just died. For the non-autistic individual such news becomes so overwhelming because there was no warning and the news completely blindsided them. Reactions of "This can't be true," "I just talked to them yesterday," or "There must be some mistake" dominate their thoughts. Disbelief isn't the same as denial to me. Denial is a state of mind where the person refuses to accept the fact that someone has died. It can last days, weeks, or even longer. Disbelief is what I believe is a state of mind that readies the brain for processing such a heavy loss. It disengages the mind from focusing on the mundane tasks of daily life by mentally sorting through all the information to verify the reality of the situation. It is a very transient short-lived phase. For the autistic individual, disbelief is almost nonexistent. Because the news is a fact, our logical brain accepts that as real and immediately tends to skip right into the shock phase.

For the non-autistic person, once the news is processed in the brain as being real, shock takes over. Some individuals go numb, where they are unable to feel any emotion at all. They may become stoic in demeanor and will concentrate solely on the physical aspects of the funeral arrangement. Some will freely shed tears and focus on how the death will impact those who will be affected by it. Few may become inconsolable as they immediately feel the absence of the person who has died. Others will seek solace in their religious belief system. Some will become so devastated by the realization that they are unable to function their way through the day. Generally this is the initial first phase period where the non-autistic mind looks at the "overall picture" of how that loss will impact the rest of their life. There is a tendency for them to reflect with sympathy on how someone's death will impact the deceased person's entire family and friends.

For the person with autism, the shock can be profound. The initial dominating thoughts will focus on if the death will cause a break or loss of their routine. In my case this happened when I went to the emergency room with Will and his wife when he became suddenly and violently ill the day after he and I did an autism presentation. Our conversation on the way home from that presentation the night before had focused on a scheduled speaking engagement we were committed to doing the following week, along with what we would do when we got together later that week. For the last five years I had spent every Tuesday afternoon with him and we had our routines of errands and activities we did together. The emergency room visit was on a Monday. As soon as we received the news that he had leukemia and needed to be immediately admitted to the hospital for extensive chemotherapy treatments, I was overcome by shock. Immediately my thoughts focused on if he and I were still going to do our presentation the following week and what would happen to our usual routine time together the following day.

The autistic need for self-preservation

It is absolutely imperative that you understand the innate autistic mindset of "It's all about me." Even for those autistic individuals who have been programmed to override that mindset or may not be afflicted as deeply by it as others, devastating news of any sort could cause a reversion back to this basic precept. In order to feel safe and secure, our lives are one continuous cycle of rituals and routines. Routines and rituals create within us a sense of order in a world we perceive as chaotic. They help keep us calm and they aid in controlling our anxiety. Anything (and I mean anything) that causes a break or deviation in a routine is recognized as extremely stressful and almost unfathomable. Being of a logical problem-solving mindset, our initial concerns will be centered on the stability of our routines as opposed to the emotional ramifications of losing someone through death.

Our first thoughts revolve around whether that person's death will bring an immediate interruption in our established routines. One mother told me during one of my seminars that her husband and her adult autistic son had planned for weeks to go on a weekend fishing trip with some relatives. Her son had Asperger syndrome and lived at home with his parents. The day before the big trip, the father collapsed at work from a sudden heart attack and died. When the mother broke the news to her son, all he did was "obsess" on still wanting to go on this fishing trip as scheduled. He had just lost his father but his entire focus was on "What about the fishing trip?" and who was going to take him since his father couldn't.

I have heard from other parents who have had similar reactions by their autistic child after hearing the news of the death of a family member or close friend. To the non-autistic world, our attention to established routines instead of the deceased person comes across as "insensitive." Just about everything I have read on our apparent insensitivity portrays us as unable to emotionally connect either with others or the situation at hand. That is a myth! We aren't insensitive at all. Our priority is always on ensuring our established routines remain unbroken. Those needs must be tended to before we can even begin to "feel" on an emotional level the ramifications of someone's death. It happens automatically without any conscious effort in our mind.

Immediately after receiving the news of Will's illness, it was a knee-jerk reaction for me to concentrate on what was going to happen to our routine. Here my closest friend in the world was looking at how his terminal illness was going to impact his life, while I focused on whether we would still see each other the next day as usual, and could we still do our presentation the following week. I didn't do it deliberately; it just happened. Remember what I said in Chapter 1 about our priority when faced with a crisis; our thoughts center on problem solving first. So for the autistic child or adult, who communicates their concerns about established routines being in jeopardy instead of focusing on the death at hand, understand that this isn't insensitivity per se, but just the way our brains are wired.

Indifference to the news of someone's death or national tragedy

We autistics tend to emotionally react strongly when we feel our routines are threatened. Our foremost concerns center around insulating us from the effects that change will bring to our established routines. Our reaction is directly related to what degree the deceased person was part of our routine and how much contact we had with them. Obviously the closer the relationship, the greater the disruption to our routines will be felt. The death of someone who doesn't normally interact with us and isn't part of any of our routines won't be seen as a threat to our established routines. Be it distant relative, outer circle acquaintance, or neighbor down the street, if there is no direct connection to us, then we probably won't react much if at all. There may even be a tendency not to be fazed by the death at all, with no apparent concern for the loss. The same principle can be applied to national tragedies or disasters. If it happens far away and doesn't directly impact our autistic life, then our brain tells us that there is no need for alarm or concern. Our brain functions more on the logical aspect of things as opposed to the emotional side of things.

In the wake of a national tragedy in December 2012 revolving around an elementary school shooting by a 20-year-old gunman where many children died, I was asked by a number of people what my "feelings" were regarding the incident. The United States seems to be caught up in the heated emotional debate regarding what measures should be undertaken to prevent such a tragedy from ever occurring again. Honestly, I do feel a sense of empathy for those who lost a child or loved one in that massacre, but the incident isn't foremost in my mind. Because I am not directly affected I am more concerned about maintaining stability in my little world. I understand that this action is a horrible crime and that some government action is necessary in regards to the current gun laws we have in the United States. It isn't that I don't care about what happened; I just don't have an emotional response. I have a logical response based on facts.

I have had the opportunity to discuss this tragedy with some fellow autistic adults. Universally we all felt the same way; we understood it to be a criminal act, we felt a sense of empathy to those directly involved, but after that because the tragedy didn't personally affect our life, our attention shifted back to our own lives and needs. I must reiterate this extremely important point; our indifference is based not on the inability to feel emotions, rather our response is based on how directly we are impacted by a death or tragedy. Many people with autism have an automatic emotional disconnect from others hardwired in their neurological makeup.

Indifference presenting itself as unacceptable

I was approached by a mother of an autistic child who had a question regarding an inappropriate social response by her autistic son regarding her recent miscarriage. Her son was ten years old when she found out she was pregnant again. Both parents sat him down and explained to him that he was going to have a baby sister in a few months. They laid out the changes that would occur once the baby arrived. The son asked a few questions and accepted the news without complaint. During the second trimester, however, the mother miscarried. Of course she was devastated and deeply grieved the loss of her unborn child. The father sat down with the son to explain what had happened and that the baby had died. After the son understood what happened, he showed no emotion, wanting only to resume his playtime. That night at dinner the mother broke down in tears. Her autistic son looked at her and said, "I don't know why you are crying. The baby wasn't even born yet so you didn't know her. Just replace her with a new one. It's not like she was part of the family."

To someone unfamiliar with autism, this son's response seems callous and insensitive. To a non-autistic person, grief over an unborn baby centers on the lost potential of that child. The grief is over the loss of what could have been. One grieves the loss of part of themselves. It is an emotional reaction. The autistic mind is logical and practical. This boy processed the miscarriage from a logical standpoint. The baby hadn't been born so technically it hadn't become part of the family in terms of daily routines. Never having seen nor met the baby meant to him that there was no emotional connection to her. If his mother was so grief stricken by the loss, then it would be only logical common sense to have another baby as a replacement. In all fairness to this autistic child, he wasn't being insensitive. He processed the miscarriage from a logical problem-solving point of view. Remember I said that the autistic mindset looks first at problem solving when it comes to dealing with issues.

In another case, a parent of an autistic teenager came up to me looking for clarity over his daughter's "insensitive" reaction over the sudden death of a classmate of hers. A teenage boy died as the result of being involved in a car crash. Other classmates were crying over the news. The cause of the crash was the result of him texting and driving at the same time. When the father asked his daughter what her feelings were about this tragedy, she shrugged her shoulders in apparent indifference and said, "Well, what do you expect when you do something that is so stupid and against the law?"

While initially this seems like an awful response, she was just processing what happened through the filter of logic and not emotion. She spoke the truth in a very blunt manner. This doesn't mean that she may not have emotions attached to the death, it only means that initially autistic individuals tend to process events logically before emotionally. Emotions are there and will surface once the logical aspects are sufficiently examined.

Emotional disconnect and detachment

Most individuals with autism are detached from their emotions, that doesn't mean that we don't have them. It means there is an emotional disconnect of displaying emotions that may contradict what it is we are actually feeling. We may not understand that the emotion which seems out of place for the situation is directly related to an unresolved issue. Some have witnessed autistic individuals displaying very inappropriate emotions such as uncontrollable laughter at a funeral, or angry outbursts at the news of someone's death. We become so busy trying to find solutions to a problem when confronted with a crisis that we can be totally oblivious to the emotions that are surfacing. They may be there but they don't register in our brains at the moment of crisis. In a sense it is as if they don't even exist to us because it is hard to make the connection that what we are feeling is the result of the crisis we are experiencing.

Take for example the child who, upon hearing that their grandparent has died, responds with "I am glad they are dead" or "I hate them." It makes no sense seeing how much they "loved" that person to be so angry. Understand that it is an emotional disconnect. The anger is just a manifestation of raw unbridled emotion of overwhelming sorrow and sadness over such a loss. There is this attempt in the autistic brain to sever emotional ties with anything that causes such distress. The individual who truly feels that anger is legitimate isn't aware that it actually isn't, and is only an emotional expression of grief.

Take the individual who is experiencing pronounced anxiety as a result of a broken routine. You would think that they would recognize what they were feeling, but they don't even if it is an intense emotional reaction. They are so hyper-focused on needing a solution to the problem at hand that they can't distract their attention away from problem solving. It is very hard for us to simultaneously multitask on a physical level, never mind on an emotional one. Our processing is focused first on how to fix the problem. Once that is dealt with, either through resolution or acceptance that there is no solution, only then does our brain turn its attention to processing emotions. The time varies from individual to individual and from one traumatic event to another. Even the autistic child or adult who at the news of a loved one's death immediately starts to wail uncontrollably, chances are it is because they are turning their attention to broken routines and scheduled events. This disconnect could last hours, days, weeks, or even months before an emotional connection is made. Usually by then there is a minor trigger of some unrelated subject that opens the floodgates to repressed emotions.

Anger as a dominant emotional response

By far the most commonly witnessed emotion in autistic spectrum disorder (ASD) individuals when confronted with the death of someone is anger. The anger initially expressed at the news of someone's death is due to the initial shock phase of sudden change. They become angry over the subconscious awareness that massive abrupt changes as a result of the loss will interrupt, disrupt, and destroy the routines which make up their world. The anger is focused over the loss of predictability and stability that will follow. Anger as an initial emotional response is almost an uncontrollable natural reaction to an overwhelming stressor that threatens to annihilate existing routines and rituals.

That being said, how anger is expressed is a learned response. There is never a valid reason for anger to manifest itself as becoming physically destructive to one's surrounding environment or physically abusive to another individual. Understand that the anger may be initially involuntary, so don't get caught up in the emotion of anger and respond back angrily. Stay calm and allow the individual to "vent" their frustration verbally. Any act of physical aggression should not be considered as harmless and overlooked. Anger that isn't managed not only is destructive but also manipulates others through fear. Unchecked anger that escalates into physical manifestations needs to be handled with anger management training.

Higher instances of meltdowns after a loss

In my consultations regarding meltdowns, I have found a sharp increase in meltdowns weeks and months after the loss of someone significant. Once a person with autism has processed completely the logical side of handling someone's death, only then does the emotional component surface. This could take weeks or months and usually presents itself as anger at the oddest of unrelated things or situations. Usually it is an overreaction to something so seemingly minor. The frustration level is very high over even the most mundane of things. For the most part the ASD individual is unable to make the connection that the frustration and anger is a delayed emotional reaction to grief.

When my friend Will broke the news to me that all our routines were suspended because he had to be admitted for chemotherapy treatment, I immediately felt this wave of anger take over; anger over the loss of our weekly visit and routines. As time went on I tried to keep some semblance of a routine going by seeing him weekly in the hospital. For five years we had a weekly routine that never wavered and now each week's visit was full of unpredictability. My visits depended on how he was feeling. There were weeks when the chemo made him too sick to have visitors. When I was there, our time together was interrupted by medical personnel checking on him as well as his other friends and family stopping by. For five years our time together was a one on one relationship and now people were popping in unexpectedly. The conversations from everyone in the room focused on multiple subjects that held no interest for me. I saw it all as an infringement of "my time" (our modified routine) with him as well as a sensory charged environment.

The stress level of trying to maintain some predictability in such a chaotic environment proved too much for me. I began to have meltdowns at the hospital which took me by surprise because I was trying so hard to control my anxiety. I had lost control of one of the most important routines in my life. The frustration and anxiety of trying to adapt to a continuously changing environment resulted in an inability to deal with ordinary things. I would come home from a visit in a foul mood. My temper flared easily over the most insignificant things. I never understood why I felt so angry all the time. I never made the connection that it was the result of Will's illness until two years after his death. It was how I emotionally processed my feelings of sorrow and grief. I was angry at him for leaving me after he promised he wouldn't. I never passed into another "stage" of grieving. Even after the anger subsided, I never cried over his death. I don't feel a desire to and I have now moved on with my life.

For many ASD individuals, meltdown reactions may increase over what normally would be considered non-issues for that person who is affected by someone's death. Their frustration level is so high from attempting to deal with the significant changes that are the result of the death. In desperation many individuals will try to fiercely protect existing routines from any slight deviations. Such a monumental task is mentally draining and as a result meltdowns will increase in areas one would least expect. Meltdowns become part of an emotional outlet to express grief because as powerful emotions surface, we don't understand them and actually fight against them causing overwhelming stress.

"I just want to be left alone"

By far one of the more perplexing autistic mannerisms revolving around problems is our apparent need to isolate ourselves from others. It is common for non-autistic individuals to seek out support of others. Having someone there to listen as they vent, offer reassuring hugs, and just knowing they aren't alone during the crisis brings a measure of comfort to the non-autistic person during the grieving process. It also seems to be a natural inclination for many non-autistic individuals to want to "be there" for someone during a loss. These gestures of solidarity are designed to reassure the grieving individual that they don't have to endure the sorrow all alone.

For an individual with autism, however, we prefer to be left alone. When I was five years old my pet cat went missing. I was extremely attached to this cat. My mother and I searched the neighborhood for her. I remember finding her lifeless body all mangled in the middle of the street. She had been hit and killed by a car. My mother stretched out her arms to me in a gesture for me to come to her to be hugged and consoled. Instead I began crying uncontrollably, running back to the house and into my room. I wanted to be left alone. It was very hard on my mother because she saw my refusal to be consoled by her as a form of rejection. That wasn't my intention. All my life I have always retreated to a private place when faced with a serious issue. I still do that now, especially upon hearing the news of a death. I find that when I am around people and I am severely stressed, I crave isolation because I can't handle interacting with them. It is too cognitively stressful.

Why do we tend to do that? It is because our brain is so wrapped up in trying to logically process what has just happened. Any outside interactions with others doesn't allow us the undivided attention required by our mind to deal with the crisis at hand. In fact, having to be around someone when our choice is to be by ourselves, will greatly increase the likelihood of a cognitive overload which will lead to a meltdown. It becomes much too difficult to effectively process our thoughts and someone else's at the same time. Especially true if the other person tries to discuss what is happening or attempts redirection by focusing on unrelated topics.

Worst of all is when a well-meaning individual attempts to console and show support by engaging in a ritual or routine with us. Doing this only increases the anxiety level because now an otherwise predictable routine or ritual which brings comfort in its "sameness" has been compromised by the participation of someone else. That person becomes an unknown variable in an otherwise stable activity bringing unpredictability to it by just their mere presence. There is no longer a calming component to engaging in that routine or ritual and now becomes another source of stress.

When some ASD individuals become extremely agitated, their senses heighten tremendously. Touch of any sort which normally would be tolerated now becomes unbearable. Even just talking or having to visually look at someone may be too overstimulating on a sensory level. Powerful emotions like sadness that manifests itself as tears could become a sensory trigger to someone with autism. Being in the same room or area with others crying could be too much of a sensory stimulating environment. In some cases the tears that flow from an autistic individual may produce such overstimulation within them that they need to isolate into a sensory deprived environment.

Distressing news of any sort creates a state of heightened anxiety. As part of our innate self-calming strategies, we autistics will seek comfort in engaging in our special interests alone. It allows us the escape from reality into a world that brings deep satisfaction and a sense of calm. Engaging in our special interest during this time is very emotionally and mentally soothing. It gives our mind a break from obsessing on the "what now" aspect of how the death will impact us on a physical level.

Sentimentality and the lack of it

By nature many non-autistic people tend to be sentimental creatures. Especially when a loved one dies, there is a need to hold on to a reminder of the deceased person, which seems to bring some measure of comfort. Having a keepsake from the deceased person has been explained to me as a way of keeping a physical part of the person's existence close to them, for example wearing the watch of someone close who has passed away. People build both makeshift and elaborate shrines as a symbolic gesture of remembrance. It is common to revisit the gravesite and talk to the grave as if the deceased person could hear what was being said. Looking at photo albums and reminiscing about the past is also very sentimental. These expressions of sentimentality are an innate part of the non-autistic mindset. It helps them feel connected to the dearly departed in an emotional sense. Reminiscing about the past brings with it a sense of emotional satisfaction and fulfillment.

For many (but not all) autistic individuals, there is no place for the emotion of sentimentality. There is a focus on living in the present without looking back at our past. Once we have accepted that someone we care about has died, we create brand new routines that no longer include them like they once did. It is a practical approach and the only way for us to move forward. There is this overall feeling of it being pointless and fruitless to reminisce about what once was but forever no longer can be. I always say that reminiscing about past memories of the deceased is like a powerful narcotic that could become addictive. Granted the non-autistic mind bristles at this comment, but it holds true not only for me but many other autistic individuals as well.

I have very few family photos and am not one to take photos of human milestones and celebrations such as birthdays, anniversaries, or holidays. Friends who have visited me always remarked on the absence of any family photographs anywhere on display in the house. I don't believe in displaying them as I can't see a purpose for it other than sentimentality. I do have a few photos on display of my husband in full combat gear taken in Viet Nam where he served, but those photos are part of my Viet Nam war military collectibles section. If my husband were to die tomorrow I would still keep them on display because of the historical significance of them and not for any sentimental reason.

The memory book

In my research on what was written about autism and grieving, I found that every article on the subject advocated the creation of a "memory book." This is a book that is created in memory of the deceased person and is filled with photos and keepsakes which "keep the memory alive" and is supposed to help the autistic individual with grieving. It is something one should do together with the autistic person as a way of helping them overcome their loss. If this is something that you know the autistic person in your life would like, then by all means explore this journey of sentimentality. My concern is that it will become adopted as a universal coping strategy for all autistic individuals. Many ASD people will not handle this memory book well.

Sometimes this lack of "nostalgia" is partly due to the logical aspect in which we perceive the world, but also it is a way of not having to deal with dwelling on the loss. We are human and have memories like everyone else. Looking back at reminders of the special happy routines we had with the deceased person only creates a deep longing to restore those routines. It brings up feelings of frustration that we can't return to those routines so we conclude logically that the practical thing to do is move forward with life without looking back. For some of us this means that we need to remove any physical evidence of the deceased person from our view. My stepfather had brought me back a beautifully hand-embroidered coat while stationed in Korea in the 1980s.

After he died I had to pack it away in a trunk along with every other reminder of him. It took years before I was able to wear that coat again. By then new routines established themselves and I moved on with life. When I wear the coat today I admire the workmanship and am thankful of the gift he had given me all those years ago. The coat doesn't conjure up memories of our times together. It is just a coat now. I did the same thing when Will died. It was only three years later that I brought out some of the trinkets I packed away that he had given me as gifts over the years. I appreciate the gifts and admire how nicely they fit in with my decor. I have all new routines that have replaced the ones I once had with him, so looking at those gift items doesn't conjure up feelings of frustration and anger over lost precious routines.

Many people with autism will have this same outlook and will begin to refuse to take part in memorials or want any connection to the deceased person. Please don't force them to embrace sentimentality when the loss of someone significant in their life is fresh. I recommend that you take those keepsakes or memory book and place them in a safe place until such a time when the autistic individual is able to accept them without issue. It may take many months and even years but please be patient and don't force the issue prematurely. Don't be offended if some ASD individuals never want any connection to the deceased person again.

When emotions do surface

I wish I could give you definitive guidelines on what emotions will be expressed and the time frames for them, but I can't. Typically in autism there is a delayed emotional reaction that varies from person to person. Some may be in touch with their emotions very shortly after receiving distressing news. Others may take weeks or months. There will come a point when tears will flow. Our culture has put unwritten time frames on the period of mourning. Leave of absences from work vary from a few days to a week or month at most. There is this assumption that life must resume as normally as possible after the funeral. I have a non-autistic friend who lost her husband over a year ago. She is still deeply in mourning yet her adult children and other family members feel that isn't normal. They are puzzled as to why she hasn't been able to "move on with life." Like it or not, there are societal expectations placed upon the period of mourning.

For a person with autism it may well be after the six month or year mark that they are hit with profound sadness and actually begin grieving the loss on an emotional level. There is usually a trigger that acts as a catalyst. Sadness, despair, longing, and obsessing about the deceased person will be a common presentation of an emotional response to the grieving process. Developing an aversion to anything that reminds them of the deceased person is also an emotional response to the intense sense of loss felt inside. If it is just too emotionally painful to process, the autistic mind will attempt to sever any emotional attachment to the deceased person.

The most effective way to help us process death emotionally is to allow us to engage in our self-soothing techniques regardless if it doesn't conform to the societal expectations of mourning. Giving us space to be alone instead of forcing us to be around others during the period from death to burial is an act of mercy towards us. Our isolation is not a statement of being antisocial, but rather a craving just to process our thoughts without interruption. A gathering of mourners can become an overstimulating sensory environment from which we need a reprieve. Our apparent responses of indifference should not be taken as an insult, but seen as just part of the autistic mindset.

If we cry and want to be held, then hold us. If we cry and want to be left alone, respect that need and give us space. Be there for us to listen when we are finally ready to discuss someone's death, even if it is months or some cases years later. Don't be alarmed if some of us never shed a tear and seem to move forward with life without too much of an emotional response. Remember that there is no one standard for how to grieve, and don't place societal expectations of what is either appropriate or "normal" for expressing grief.

CHAPTER 3

Cultural Expectations and Autism

In our western culture there are certain expectations when it comes to the death experience. From the bedside of the dying, to the wake, funeral, burial, or memorial service, there are social norms that are usually observed. There are unwritten rules for attendance, what to say, how to dress, and how to behave at such functions. To complicate matters further, religious and environmental upbringing will influence the funeral protocol. People's expectations for the appropriate observance of all present in the funeral party very often overshadow the issues an autistic individual will encounter. There will be sensory, cognitive, and social challenges to overcome for the person with autism, whether they are a child or an adult. For those unfamiliar with autism the actions and behaviors of someone with autism will be misinterpreted as disrespectful.

A case example: the death of my stepfather

My stepfather died in 1991 at the age of 46, when I was 30 years old. At that time I didn't have a diagnosis of autism. To everyone I interacted with, including my husband and relatives, I was seen as eccentric, stubborn, too rigid in thinking, and too obsessive in my actions. I came across as controlling as everything had to be and go my way. Although I was unaware that I was autistic, I was totally aware that I was different and that I didn't connect with others, no matter how hard I tried. It seemed I would always end up unconsciously sabotaging my best efforts to fit in. In hindsight I realize that it wasn't sabotage at all, but it was just my autistic behaviors and actions to deal with sensory and cognitive overloads when overly stressed that were misperceived.

My father left my mother and I when I was young and preferred not to establish a loving relationship with me thereafter. It was my stepdad who was present during the rest of my childhood and into adult years, seeing as I lived at home until I was 26 years old. To be truthful we never got along and used to fight like cats and dogs. My mother always lamented that he and I were too much alike and that we quarreled more like brother and sister as opposed to father and daughter. My stepdad was your classic Aspie. With a brilliant mind he was an electrical engineer working in the defense sector designing missiles, and he also worked in the NASA space program. This was amazing considering he had only a high school education and no college. Despite his genius, he not only seriously lacked basic social skills but also would fly into a rage whenever his routines were disrupted. Looking back at our relationship I see now that most of the time we argued over autistic points of contentions such as whose routines were more important, special interest time constraints, and whose narrow minded viewpoints over the authoritative boundaries of stepparent and stepchild were correct. Still, despite the constant bickering we did manage to find compatibility while living under the same roof.

My stepfather was diagnosed with stage four melanoma cancer shortly after my mother had met him. The doctors said he was beyond any cancer treatments as his cancer was too advanced. Given only six months to live, he married my mother. That was the beginning of my issues with him. From my vantage point I couldn't logically understand why someone close to death would even consider getting married. It was an absolute exercise in futility. Why bother? I could not understand how my mother felt it was the compassionate thing to do. I was angry at her for even proposing such a notion because it would create a legal nightmare for my mother when he died. It wasn't practical to plan a wedding and a funeral at the same time. It was a very difficult time for me as all my routines and rituals were shattered by the unpredictability brought on by his illness.

Amazingly he survived the first six months, and then another six months, and then a year followed by another year. Although he was prone to long recuperations in bed from something minor such as a cold, he beat the odds and didn't die. There were many scares along the way but life resumed as normal for the three of us. He went into remission and after the eight year mark, he was officially considered "cured" of his cancer. All thoughts of death and dying were erased from our minds. He escorted me up the aisle at my wedding in 1987 and actually logically convinced my mother that my husband's and my moving to another state to pursue farming wasn't as foolish as she felt it was. In 1989 he and my mother considered relocation close to our farm.

Before any real steps were made towards this goal, he started to not feel good. He had problems with forgetfulness and his speech was becoming sluggish. Numerous trips to the doctors and a battery of tests concluded he was cancer free and the doctors felt that he had contracted some sort of viral infection. In February of 1991 he was hospitalized because he was becoming belligerent and so forgetful that he was unsafe to be left alone. Every test came back negative for his cancer so we all were under the impression that whatever he had would eventually go away. I never visited him while he was in the hospital because my mother expressly asked me not to come because of his deteriorated mental state. She told me to wait until he recovered some day. The last week of July 1991 he slipped into a coma and the doctors felt exploratory brain surgery was the best chance for figuring out what was causing this. Neither my mother nor I were prepared for the news. During the operation the surgeon discovered that his brain was riddled with the exact type of melanoma cancer he was initially diagnosed with 12 years earlier. He never came out of the coma and died five days after the surgery on his 46th birthday.

The results of the surgery completely took me by surprise. My mother and I had never even considered his death an option up until that point. There was no plan on how to deal with his death. With no funeral prearrangements, my life was thrown into utter chaos.

My mother was unable to function and as the only child, all the arrangements fell upon my shoulders. My stepdad was an orphan so there was neither help nor support from his side of the family. My mother decided that he should be buried in my town to fulfill his last wishes of moving up to Maine to be near my husband and I. Although there would be a memorial service where she lived, the wake, funeral, and interment would occur close to my home.

Logistically this would prove to be a nightmare because by then my husband and I had a full working livestock farm. It was a rigid daily schedule that included milking cows and goats around the same time by hand twice daily as well as caring for a full complement of livestock including horses, sheep, chickens, turkeys, and pigs. This lifestyle made it impossible for both my husband and I to leave the farm for any length of time but it was a way of living that brought me such serenity and sense of accomplishment. We were always too busy to even consider socializing or making and maintaining friends outside of the farming world. My extended contact with others revolved only around farming concerns so my social skills at the time were virtually nonexistent. My conversational skills were limited to farming topics only. At the time we lived without electricity (by choice) as we embraced the simplicity of living off the land as it was done a century earlier. At the end of the day when the sun went down, all work ceased. Without the distractions of television, radio, and computers, our home was a sanctuary. The soft lighting of the oil lamps provided a sensory soothing environment. The stillness and solitude of the evening soothed away most of the sensory or cognitive stressors incurred during the day. My home is uncluttered, with even my "junk drawer" being completely organized and tidy. With an intense need for order I adhere to the motto, "A place for everything and everything in its place." The tranquility of my sanctuary however would soon be shattered with the arrival of the funeral guests, most of whom would be staying at my home.

Since my mother and stepdad lived a good seven hours away from us, it was expected that I open up my home for overnight guests who traveled long distances for the funeral. Their social circle consisted of dentists, lawyers, CEOs, and those involved in the high tech industry at upper management levels. These people immersed themselves in city culture and amenities. They viewed my lifestyle as ridiculous and saw me as perhaps afflicted with some mental illness that would cause this intense desire to want to withdraw from the "real" world. I had people sleeping in just about every room and some on the floor. There was only one bathroom for all of us with limited running water. Refrigeration consisted of a root cellar and an ice box designed for two people and not 20. There was no air conditioning or fans to provide relief from the hot humid August days or nights.

With no artificial entertainment at night (television), there was a continual social interaction between all of us until bedtime. With such extreme diversity in lifestyles, it was a struggle to find topics of mutual interest. The sensory stimulation was so unbearable, I would continually excuse myself under the guise that my livestock animals needed special attention. I would retreat to the quiet of the barn just to escape the feeling of impending doom from too much sensory and cognitive overload. The guests in my house were touching and handling my antiques and things without permission and never putting them back exactly as they found them. Their personal items were scattered in disarray all over the house. The continued questions of why I found such a primitive and austere life fulfilling became draining. On top of having to deal with my home being invaded by guests for the weekend, I was in charge of all funeral arrangements, as well as looking after my mother, who struggled just to get up in the morning.

The morning of the wake was very chaotic. Having to provide breakfast for a large number of people was daunting. Surviving in an overly sensory stimulated environment without relief was taking its toll on me. On top of that the funeral director called and said he couldn't find the slacks that went with my stepfather's burial suit and unless we provided them quickly, there would be no viewing of the body at the wake. Since my stepdad was always a practical joker I thought this scenario was extremely funny and I couldn't stop laughing because I knew that he would find this just as funny if he were still alive. Although my mother understood my laughter, everyone else viewed my laughter as totally inappropriate.

I so desperately craved a sensory deprived environment that I balked at having to go to the wake. Thank God my mother insisted that I not go because she wanted me to remember him as he looked in better times and not as the gaunt, unrecognizable man that cancer turned him into. I stayed home as everyone else including my husband went to the wake. I have no regrets to this day for that decision. I needed to be alone so that I could engage in my daily routines without interruptions. Well-intentioned guests offered to assist me with my chores. But by the time I got done explaining how something should be done and watching them fumble incorrectly doing it, it took twice as long. Something as simple as someone washing the dishes but then putting them away in the wrong locations became very frustrating for me.

I know by now some of you are wondering what role my husband played during this time. My husband and I married for practical concerns and not so much for romantic love. I am by nature not an emotionally nurturing or giving person, and he in turn as a combat war veteran tends to be emotionally distant. We have a wonderful symbiotic relationship because of this and in 2012 we celebrated our 25th wedding anniversary. He knows that when I am stressed, depressed, or grieving that I need to be left alone. He will tend to take over some of my physical tasks just to give me extra "alone time" to deal with the crisis at hand. During the period of having guests stay at our house, he was the host who entertained them. Knowing full well my frequent trips to the barn was the result of my inability to cope with the guests, he graciously explained how tending livestock would require my periodic absences. My husband had witnessed numerous sensory and cognitive meltdowns in the four years we were married without understanding what they were. He just knew that it was better to manipulate the environment to reduce my stress level rather than having him endure the experience of another one of my meltdowns. He didn't demand that I participate in the formalities of the wake and funeral.

The morning of the funeral my mother and I talked about my stepdad. She told me that he would want us to be happy for him and not cry. She asked me to remember him with laughter and not tears. To her, his death meant just a passing into a new heavenly existence devoid of all pain and suffering. I asked her if he would mind if I wore my brightly colored Hawaiian print shirt instead of the traditional black clothing worn at funerals in honor of his going to a happier place. After all, if his wish is for us to remember him as happy, a loudly colored printed shirt was more appropriate than a dreary black one. My mother smiled and said that wearing the Hawaiian shirt would be something he would have wanted me to do, so I did.

I was the only one in the entire funeral party not dressed in black. Naturally the guests once again looked upon my outfit negatively. I was even asked by some of them why I chose to be disrespectful to the deceased person with my flamboyant attire. Looks of disdain were cast my way and I began to feel intimidated. It was clear that I failed miserably in meeting the societal fashion requirement for funeral wear. If that wasn't bad enough, the stress of being out of my routines combined with the continuous sensory overload created such a heightened state of anxiety I was unable to join the funeral procession to the cemetery for the service. As the last car drove away, I knew that the guests didn't think very favorably of my conduct and decision to stay behind. The only way I could self-regulate my anxiety at the time was to isolate myself and spend time rocking and listening to music. This helped me calm down greatly. Luckily the cemetery was less than three miles away, so once I pulled myself together, I hopped on my bicycle and peddled my way there in the stifling heat.

I hadn't missed more than five or ten minutes of the service. The humidity combined with physical exhaustion and mental fatigue took its toll on my body. Feeling weak I rationalized that my stepfather wouldn't mind if I just sat down at the edge of his grave to listen to the remainder of the service. The minister in his sermon reminded us all to reflect on the happy memories we had with my stepfather. Everyone else was standing. The moment was solemn and somber. My mother and some of the guests were crying silently. Trying not to be overwhelmed by the sorrow being expressed, I focused on the minister's instructions to remember the good times I had with my stepfather. Despite his genius IQ, my stepfather lacked utter and complete common sense. This led to many awkward but hilarious moments when he was alive which flooded my memory, causing me to smile and chuckle under my breath. So there I sat at the edge of the grave in my loudly colored shirt smiling and snickering while everyone else stood with stoic expressions on their face. Glances of utter disgust were sent my way. My behavior was seen as so disrespectful and inappropriate that to this day some of those people still refuse to talk to me. I wasn't willfully trying to be disrespectful. I was only following the wishes of my mother not to be sad, and the instruction of the minister to remember the fond memories.

It wasn't that I had no feelings, or that I didn't take the situation seriously; hosting the funeral was so demanding that I was in a constant problem-solving mode. I expended all my mental resources trying to maintain some semblance of my routines amidst the chaos of having people I hardly knew in my home for an extended visit. To everyone in the funeral party (except my mother and husband, who accepted my uniqueness) I failed miserably when it came to the cultural expectations of what was appropriate behavior for a funeral. My hyper-focusing on the practical aspects of daily farm life combined with an apparent lack of appropriate emotions for someone in mourning was misinterpreted by the funeral attendees. I was seen as someone who deliberately decided to ignore the social custom of the day regarding someone's death. Sadly, cultural expectations often exclude the needs of a person with autism. There are some special considerations to keep in mind if you have an autistic individual in your funeral party.

IN HINDSIGHT

Had I known that I was autistic I would have approached his passing much differently. So much time and emotional expectation went into the eventual move close by of my mother and stepfather. There was no alternative or "plan B" in case that script failed. The doctors felt confident he would recover from his illness. I should have begun as soon as he was hospitalized to develop an alternate script of what to do should he die. His death caught me completely by surprise. Instead of hosting the funeral party at my home, I would have offered to help find them lodging in nearby motels. I needed solitude. Having a house full of guests didn't allow for proper de-stressing strategies, because the social expectations to play the part of a welcoming hostess was all encompassing and time consuming. *Everyone* who would be in attendance would be informed that I have autism, with special accommodations put in place to get through the entire grieving process. If the guests knew and understood that I was autistic, I am confident that my funeral attire and behaviors wouldn't have come across as offensively as they did.

Cultural expectations: special considerations for a person with autism when handling a wake, funeral, or memorial service

Attending any gathering may prove difficult for some people with autism under normal circumstances. When the gathering revolves around the death of someone, there are extra challenges to keep in mind when you have an autistic individual in attendance. There are so many unwritten rules for conduct at wakes, funerals, and memorial services that are expected to be followed. Many people with autism may be unfamiliar with these unwritten rules and not be aware of how to conduct themselves at such functions. For some people with autism, the challenges of attending such a function would be too great for them to bear. Even if the individual ordinarily has little or no difficulties with social gatherings, under these circumstances that could change. The stressors of unpredictability and breaks or loss of routines brought on by someone's death can severely hamper self-regulatory behaviors of a person with autism.

BEING FAMILIAR WITH THE AUTISTIC INDIVIDUAL

The golden rule of thumb here is to know your client, child, sibling, friend, or spouse with autism. Be familiar with their sensory and cognitive triggers as well as know what their limits are when in public. The most common mistake is to force a person with autism to extend beyond their coping limits within a sensory charged environment. Triggers and limits vary from individual to individual. Some people with autism may have no trouble staying for the entire length of the wake or funeral while others may not be able to stay very long or attend at all. If you encounter severe resistance from an autistic individual in regards to attending such a gathering, really evaluate if it is in the best interest to force that person to go. Also remember that there is no single approach that works with autism. Every book written including mine are generally guides that offer practical solutions but may not be applicable to everyone with autism. Don't force an "approach" to meet the cultural expectations surrounding someone's passing just because you read about it in a book on autism or grieving. Stay within the comfort limits of the person with autism. *Make sure that everyone involved in the funeral proceedings understands that there will be an autistic individual in attendance.* Educate them on what to expect from that autistic individual and what special allowances will be needed for them.

LOOKING AT SENSORY TRIGGERS

Many times simple sensory triggers tend to be overlooked. For instance, particularly at wakes, there may be lots of fresh pungent flowers. Because it is a social gathering, there will be a tendency for men and women to wear perfume or cologne. If the wake is being held at a funeral home, the smells of the building could be a factor. Some people with autism have such a heightened sense of smell that they can detect the faint scent of embalming fluid emanating from the deceased person. At the gravesite for the funeral service, the smell of earth and dirt may also be a factor.

Inclement weather for someone with autism can be a sensory issue. Personally, I cannot tolerate snowflakes or raindrops on my face. I avoid exposing myself to such intense sensory triggers. For some people with autism, bright sunlight is a sensory trigger for their eyesight. Know in advance of attending if the autistic individual has any sensory aversions that may be encountered.

Tactile issues must also be considered. Can the autistic individual handle wearing a suit or dress or clothing not normally worn? My concern would be for those with severe sensory issues regarding clothing. Can they handle wearing fabrics that they normally don't wear? What if they flatly refuse to wear appropriate funeral attire like a suit and tie or a dress or pant suit? Evaluate whether it is prudent to stick to the cultural expectations of dressing appropriately. For the person with autism who dresses a certain way daily, for how long are they able to cope with wearing something not usually worn?

Extended human contact is usually expected during these times. Long hugs, handshakes, kisses, rubbing someone's back, and placing of hands on shoulders are very common. In the non-autistic world for the most part, human touch during such times brings a measure of comfort. For a person with autism, touch is a very delicate and personal issue. Some individuals cannot tolerate certain forms of touching including hugs. Even if the individual could tolerate hugging, how much hugging would be too much? Others, particularly younger autistic children, may have an excessive need for "bear hugs" (deep pressure hugs) from one person or from whomever they have contact with. It is one thing to give another person a hug, but if the autistic individual had to reciprocate numerous times within the limited time span of the gathering, it could turn into an aversion resulting in a sensory overload.

Sound is another sensory factor. Music playing in the background, even if it is soft, may present an issue for some individuals on the spectrum. Groups of people talking or whispering, or the frequent sound of doorbells and doors opening and closing, could become distressing. Chairs moving, especially if they are of the metal folding type, can quickly become irritating to someone sensitive to sounds. Sometimes silence can be very distressing for some individuals on the spectrum. How loud is the noise level of the social function? Can they sit or stand quietly for the duration of the service? Would their need to get up and wander around be seen as disruptive to others?

Visual overstimulation from too many colors and types of flowers may make the area very visually "busy." Bright shiny jewelry objects accentuated by black clothing could become a visual distraction. Lots of displayed photos of the deceased person may be very visually stimulating. What type of lighting is being used in the room where the viewing, service, or social gathering afterwards is conducted? Fluorescent lights pose a problem for visual sensory overload for many individuals on the spectrum. Sometimes the bountiful refreshment and buffet tables can create a visual distraction if they are viewable from the setting area of the service. Loud print carpets and wallpapers can also create a visual sensory overload as well as interfere with depth perception, causing frequent stumbling when walking in that area.

USING APPROPRIATE CONVERSATIONAL SKILLS

There are certain cultural expectations when it comes to interpersonal interactions before, during, and immediately after the wake and funeral. Topics of conversation are generally focused on fond remembrances of the deceased person with immediate family members. Personal conversations revolving around anything but the dearly departed with others are generally muted and kept low key. It is customary to extend some sort of condolence to those directly affected by the death of a loved one or friend, and to offer either moral or physical support. It is not the time for rambling monologues on special interest topics. What is the conversational skill level of the individual with autism in attendance? How will they react to receiving condolences from others? If the person with autism lost a close relative or friend, can they tolerate listening to conversations about that deceased person? Are they able to offer phrases of condolences to those mourning the loss of a loved one? How do you inform those in the funeral party not to trigger conversations accidently that will launch the autistic individual into an inappropriate rambling monologue?

BEING AWARE OF CLOSE PROXIMITY TO PEOPLE

One area that may be overlooked is the collective emotional state of the social gathering. So many autistic individuals are highly attuned to the emotional states of the people close by. This is especially true of non-verbal individuals who seem to "sense" emotions of distress. I have had countless teachers share with me that when a non-verbal child begins to spiral into a meltdown, the other autistic children in the class also begin to become anxious. They are keenly aware of the level of anxiety within the room. If the anxiety develops into a full-blown meltdown without swift de-escalation measures, soon the other autistic children within the class spiral into meltdowns also.

During the viewing hours of the wake, many people take one last look at the deceased person. This stirs up powerful emotions of loss and sadness. Will the crying and wailing of people in the room (or during the funeral service) cause the person with autism to become anxious? In certain individuals with autism, their inability to relate to or understand crying will tend to trigger emotions of frustration and possibly even anger. Sometimes the crying of others will cause the autistic individual to burst into tears.

Particularly in the non-verbal individual, their distress at being exposed to this may cause them to erupt into loud vocalizations or possibly even screaming or crying. The emotional level of the gathering may be too intense for some on the spectrum, causing them to run from the room or gathering, whether they are non-verbal or high functioning. Sometimes in the verbal autistic population, someone's crying and sadness may create an intense level of stress because the autistic individual doesn't have a social script that deals with handling other people's grief. This could lead to a panic response, which may lead to either a heightened state of anxiety or the person bolting out of the room or area.

STIMMING THAT IS OBVIOUS TO OTHERS

Having to sit through a wake, funeral, or memorial service is unpleasant for most people but for the autistic individual it could tax their limit in so many ways. Stimming is a coping strategy employed by everyone with autism as a means to control anxiety. Stimming will vary from individual to individual but rocking is the most commonly seen stim behavior when stressed in both non-verbal and higher functioning individuals. Humming, vocalizations, jumping, hand flapping, and other obvious forms of stimming may become intense under these circumstances. Generally we (autistics) like to isolate ourselves when stressed so if the autistic individual is confined within the social gathering, how will the flagrant stimming impact others in the group setting? What if the stimming behavior takes over and the individual becomes unable to stop or engage with others?

Helpful strategies to assist the autistic individual with cultural expectations

The best way to assist an autistic person in handling the cultural expectations during a burial process is by utilizing a script or plan designed especially for such an event. Ideally this should be prepared well in advance of someone's death, but that isn't always possible. Still it is a good idea to start to scrutinize the potential areas of difficulties such an event will cause the autistic person in your life. When death hits a family, especially a sudden death, the shock will be so overwhelming that many times confusion and bewilderment cloud the judgment of those directly affected. The special needs of a person with autism may become overshadowed by concentrating on arranging funeral preparations by the parents or caregivers. For the average person there is a certain level of acceptance and expectation that their daily routine will be disrupted by such an event. For the autistic individual, however, they will not be as accepting or gracious about disruptions to their routines or planned events.

FAMILIARIZING THE INDIVIDUAL
WITH THE LOCATION

Social stories can be an invaluable tool for creating a mental picture of the site of the funeral proceedings but don't use it as the sole strategy. I advocate not only using actual photos of the locations but also visiting these places in advance of the actual event, even if it is only a day or two in advance. This allows the autistic individual to become familiar with the environment, thereby reducing an unknown (the environment) and also familiarizing them with the sensory impacts of such a location. Giving us a visual of the surroundings affords us to mentally map out our physical position within that location. It is a major aid to the self-scripting process within our brains for a new activity or event. If this isn't a possibility, I strongly recommend that someone videotape a walk-through tour of the location so that the autistic person at least has a virtual video tour of the area prior to attending.

Becoming familiar with the surroundings will aid the autistic person in providing some predictability in an otherwise unfamiliar setting. Every little bit will help in reducing the anxiety level that accompanies the unknown. Familiarization with the actual surroundings before the gathering takes place also allows for the detection of unforeseen sensory triggers. Keep in mind that even if the individual under normal circumstances can tolerate a sensory stimulating environment, during a time of upheaval and broken routines, sensory non-issues could become sensory overload triggers.

DISCUSSING IN DETAIL WHAT TO EXPECT

Again this is where a social story will be helpful. Give the autistic person a detailed itinerary of what will occur during the ceremony time wise, tell them who will be attending, and what appropriate behaviors and conduct will be required of them. Don't just lecture and expect the individual to process it without question. Ask for feedback from the autistic individual on their interpretation of what is expected. Chances are that they won't be able to understand this initially. This entire topic will create anxiety so don't attempt to go through the whole lesson all at once. Allow time for them to process what is being expected. Break it down into smaller lessons and allow them to ask questions. Offer them stim tools to control their stress level if you see it rising during the discussion.

CREATING A TIME FRAME AND SETTING TIME LIMITS

To an autistic individual following a script and adhering to a well-defined timeline are extremely important. Scripts and routines are two of the most important things in our life. Since this is a time of intense unpredictability, creating a script of what will be occurring is extremely important in bringing a sense of order to the chaos at hand. I am a big believer in visual reminders that help me in maintaining my routines. Whenever I attend any sort of social function, I create a written agenda that scripts out my timeline for that event. I carry it in my pocket, which reassures me that I have a viable script to follow should I at any time become nervous or anxious during that event. Have such an agenda on paper as a visual aid. Create a timeline of what will occur for each day, when, and for how long.

Communicate clearly concrete time frames for arriving, attending, and leaving the function. Don't decide to modify or change the times abruptly or without communicating that clearly in advance. Even though this is an extraordinary event where you may want to stay beyond the time limit set, don't! The person with autism is depending on you to follow the script completely and without deviation. Your following along with the script brings to them a sense of structure which they desperately are craving. Arrive and leave at the pre-chosen times.

One of the more common reasons for meltdowns revolves around not following defined timelines. Sometimes people fail to realize that to an autistic individual, a script is written in stone. Rigidly following a script and timeline set forth within that script brings a sense of predictability and comfort. Timelines are boundaries that separate the various daily scripts in our head. Arriving or leaving a function earlier or later destroys the time boundary that divides the following various scripts we have in our mind. Now because of this disruption the following script is off its timeline, as will be the one after that, creating unpredictability and instability of the immediate future. This becomes very distressing to someone with autism. Even a 15 minute time disruption, which seems a non-issue with non-autistic people, can feel like a complete breakdown of a script to an autistic individual because the 15 minutes will have to be lost in some subsequent script for the day. This in turn destroys the fluidity of the scripts, which may result in the individual obsessing over which routine or event will be negatively impacted.

REHEARSING APPROPRIATE CONDOLENCE PHRASES

Don't assume even if the autistic individual is an adult that they will be aware of what the appropriately expected expressions of condolences are. I wasn't aware of such phrases until someone explained them to me after I (as an adult) attended a funeral and offered a truthful but ill-timed comment instead of a condolence to a widow. During the viewing hours of the wake of her husband, people were going up to her and offering her condolences on her loss. When it came to my turn, I told her that she was young enough and could find another replacement husband in time. While that may have been a truthful statement, the timing was inappropriate. She was grieving the loss of her husband and not in a state of mind to look into the distant future. I only gathered that I misspoke by looking at the shocked expressions of those within earshot of my comment. The widow was speechless. Of course that was before I was diagnosed with autism, so there was no understanding of where I was coming from.

Be concise as to what expressions to use. Have the individual with autism rehearse them so that they are easily remembered. Try role playing so as to get the autistic individual comfortable to know when it is the appropriate time to offer an expression of condolence and with whom. Inform them of what conversations are appropriate for the setting. Advise them on turn taking, limiting discussing special interest topics, and not interrupting conversations already in progress. Also explain the possibility of someone being so overcome with grief that they do not want to engage in lengthy conversation so they must respect their need for silence and privacy. Instruct them that being silent at times and not continually talking is a good way to show respect for the mourners and deceased person. Explain that silence allows others to quietly reflect on memories, thoughts, and feelings of the one who died.

HAVING AN EXIT STRATEGY IN CASE OF OVERWHELMING ANXIETY

Attending such an emotionally charged event may just be "the straw that breaks the camel's back." Death brings with it unanticipated lifestyle changes. Routines and scripts will disintegrate abruptly. The emotional turmoil within the household may create a state of heightened anxiety within an autistic individual. All the stress associated with someone's death will greatly tax all the coping strategies of those who are involved, whether they are autistic or not. Tolerances towards autistic mannerisms may be reduced, allowing tempers to become short.

There could come a point anywhere in the funeral proceedings where the autistic individual exceeds their social tolerance limit. This could even occur after the funeral service when everyone gathers back at someone's home or rented hall for snacks and refreshments. Develop an exit strategy that allows the autistic person to quietly leave the room or service if they feel they can't tolerate the setting any longer. Set up certain non-verbal signals an autistic individual could communicate to you in such a way that doesn't disrupt others around them to let you know that their tolerance level for that function is decreasing. Plan on bringing a variety of stim tools for them to utilize for self-soothing and anxiety reduction. Most importantly allow them to self-soothe at the first signs that they are showing anxiety of any sort. If the anxiety level continues to rise, escort the individual out of the function before it turns into a full-blown meltdown.

EVALUATING THE PRACTICALITY OF FORCING AN AUTISTIC INDIVIDUAL TO ATTEND A WAKE OR FUNERAL

There is an expectation for wakes and funerals that all family members need to attend them in order to "pay their respects" to the deceased person. My feelings are that if a person with autism expresses a desire to participate in any social function, they should be allowed to do so. This helps with social building skills. I do however have concerns regarding autistic individuals who strongly object to participating in funeral proceedings but are forced to do so anyway. For the non-autistic world, the whole funeral process helps with emotional closure. To someone with autism, emotional closure is secondary to rebuilding a new viable script or routine. Unlike any other social function in which a person with autism engages in regularly, a funeral is a very foreign and unfamiliar event that doesn't happen on a regular basis. It may just be a onetime event for a very long time. The individual's refusal may be a way of communicating that such a gathering will create a sensory or cognitive overload. If they begin to fret about attending the proceedings before actually being there, that is a sign they are mentally unequipped to deal with the stressors associated with the event.

Really evaluate why it is important for that person with autism to attend. Is it for their emotional needs or the funeral party's? Keep in mind that there will be so many changes to that person's life that their world will seem to be one unending tumultuous chain of unpredictability. Are they cognitively able to understand what is occurring around them? Will forcing them out of an established routine just to attend such a function cause more distress than necessary?

Unlike many other conditions, autism brings with it a completely different way of processing the world around them. To some individuals with autism these cultural functions surrounding death are unimportant to them and they would just as soon prefer not to participate. While it initially may seem callous and antisocial, it could also be due to the fact that such functions are too emotionally demanding for them. This is why I keep stressing that you should really understand the autistic individual in your life. Knowing their limitations, expectations, desires, and triggers will go a long way in helping you to formulate how best for them to engage in the cultural expectations of social gatherings around funerals.

Autism doesn't take a holiday for funerals. The special needs and accommodations for a person with autism can't be suspended during the planning and executing of funeral arrangements.

CHAPTER 4

Knowing What to Say

Death is a very unpleasant topic to think about. It is difficult for most people to ponder the topic of our mortality. Media ads today focus on the quest for eternal youth whether it be through cosmetics, fitness programs, or vitamin-fortified refreshments. For most people, the thought of dying and what lies "beyond the great unknown" is a subject that should remain unspoken of until that time draws near. This reluctance to embrace death as the natural order of things has led to an almost universal avoidance of the reality of death. Expressions that convey death attempt to minimize the stark reality of dying such as "passed on" or "gone to heaven." Colorful, almost humorous, euphemisms such as "taking a dirt nap" or "gone to count worms" are attempts to make death seem less foreboding.

For individuals on the autism spectrum who are extremely literal, these expressions are a virtual verbal landmine. Receiving news that a loved one has died is never easy. Attempting to cushion the blow by using well-intended phrases and expressions that do not portray the reality of death may only add to their distress. Not communicating clearly the permanence of someone's death will lead to confusion over whether that person is really dead. It is more humane to be brutally blunt the first time the news must be broken to someone with autism. This allows them to comprehend that the loss is permanent right from the beginning and will avoid you having to re-explain it time and time again.

Commonly used phrases that can be confusing to an ASD individual

The following euphemisms for death can be confusing to people with autism:

- Passed on

- Passed away

- Gone to one's reward

- Gone to heaven

- Gone to a better place

- Expired

- Gone to the afterlife

- Resting in peace

- Gone to meet one's maker

- Departed

- It was God's will

- Laid to rest

- Putting an animal to sleep

These expressions are examples of making the death seem a little bit more palatable and aren't so "concrete." No matter how much conversational skill training an autistic individual may have had, when severely stressed their brain will revert back to a literal processing mode. This means that while they may "get" everyday common expressions, when faced with an overwhelming stressful situation, their brain goes into concrete problem fixing mode. Everything becomes literal. It will be very hard to explain that Grandpa has "gone to a better place." To a child with autism, this may be interpreted as Grandpa didn't like it here and found a much better place to go thereby abandoning his grandchild. If you use an expression like "he passed on" or "he checked out" be prepared for questions about passed on or checked out to where and why? Ambiguity as to the permanence of the deceased person through such phrases will create a sense of confusion and frustration.

Timmy: a case in point

I was contacted for a consultation regarding a ten-year-old boy who had high functioning autism who we will call "Timmy." Initially the consultation was regarding a string of severe meltdowns that weren't responding to any behavioral plans. Upon further inquiry I was told that Timmy had been very close to his grandfather and had spent the afternoon with him every Sunday. The explosive meltdowns began shortly after his grandfather's death. Timmy's parents explained to him that Grandpa had gone to heaven and would always watch over him from above. Knowing how broken routines are so upsetting, Timmy's parents decided to try to maintain some semblance of his precious routine, so they decided to go to the cemetery every Sunday afternoon to bring flowers and "visit" Grandpa. They had Timmy place the flowers on the headstone and then told him that he could look at the grave and talk to Grandpa as Grandpa could hear him. At that moment Timmy spiraled into such an explosive meltdown, they had to leave the cemetery. From then on every time his parents even mentioned going back to place fresh flowers on Grandpa's grave, Timmy had a meltdown.

They had taken Timmy to a therapist, who attempted to counsel him on dealing with grief, but Timmy's meltdowns began at the slightest mention of his grandfather. This was a boy who was normally well adjusted and explosive meltdowns and severe autistic mannerisms were something they had not seen in him before. He regressed in all social skill areas and displayed extreme stimming behaviors such as continuous rocking, disruptive humming in class, and an obsessive focus on his special interest. Finally, after reading my book on meltdowns, Timmy's mother contacted me in desperation asking for any insight or help for this situation.

It didn't take very long to pinpoint the reasons for his frequent meltdowns and consequent regressive behaviors. It was due in essence to a communication discrepancy. Timmy's parents had explained to him how his grandfather was in heaven enjoying all the wonderful things he used to like to do, like fishing and playing golf. It was hard on Timmy so they went on to say that Grandpa will always be with him keeping watch over him from heaven. After a religious social story on going to heaven, Timmy began to accept the reality of the situation. Up to this point there were no behavioral issues regarding the loss.

Knowing how abrupt changes to an existing routine can be stressful, Timmy's parents decided to try to maintain the weekly Sunday afternoon routine by visiting Grandpa at the cemetery. It was well-intended but misdirected. As a rule I always advocate changes to routines be done slowly except when it comes to death.

With death there is no way a routine modification is possible if it centered on the one who died. In that case I believe the best thing to do is to deal with the abrupt ending and create an entirely new and completely different routine in its place. Timmy was used to playing catch with his grandfather and making lunch together every Sunday afternoon for the last few years. All of a sudden that allotted time frame was spent staring at a cold inanimate headstone bearing the name of his grandfather. He was used to being very interactive with his grandfather and being told to have a one-sided conversation with a tombstone wasn't very interactive at all. Timmy didn't view this time as "healing."

After interviewing numerous non-autistic people for this book, I have come to understand that frequently visiting the gravesite of a loved one helps them ease the transition of loss. To a person with autism this may not be so helpful. We need to embrace the reality that the person is gone forever and nothing will be the same. Timmy began his spiral at the gravesite because on a subconscious level it left a glimmer of hope that someday his established routine with Grandpa could be restored. Going to the cemetery was too close to the original routine and therefore didn't convey completely the finality of death.

I know this may come across as harsh and insensitive, but many non-autistic people have a tendency to assume that what works for the majority must work for everyone. People with autism aren't as emotionally inspired to engage in thoughts or actions which help nurture their internal emotional needs. We autistics tend to see things as black and white, and practical and not practical. My stepfather is buried about two miles from my farm, yet I have visited the gravesite only three times since 1991 to check on the condition of the headstone. I have no desire to go other than that: to me it is just an exercise in futility because only his decaying body remains at that plot.

The main reason Timmy developed meltdown episodes was over the confusion he was experiencing in regards to where his grandfather actually was. He was told that his grandfather was happy in heaven, probably fishing or golfing, yet he was also told to talk to him while staring down at his grave. Timmy logically couldn't process where he was; up in heaven or stuck in a coffin underneath the cold ground. Problem solving is our first inclination in dealing with issues, and Timmy was continuously becoming cognitively overloaded at the mention of his grandfather, because his brain was trying to figure out the location of his grandfather. Until he was able to find an answer to this dilemma, he couldn't focus on much else.

Being mindful of how you communicate loss to an ASD individual

The only way to avoid scenarios similar to Timmy's story is by being very succinct in the language you use. Be blunt even if that seems cold and insensitive. Don't try to ease into the conversation slowly, because that will only act as a blindside when you finally come out and say someone has died. It is best to start right out with telling the autistic individual that the person has died. It will be a shock but there will be less chance of any misinterpretations that way. Present the facts as you have them right there and then. Before actually having that conversation, be ready to offer up some solutions to the routines which will be affected, because that is generally where the first questions will stem from.

Consistency is the key to helping a person with autism understand death. Everyone involved in the funeral party and then those who work or live with the autistic individual must all use the same phrases with that person. It does no good to explain to Timmy that Grandpa has died in concrete literal terms, only to find some relative at the funeral telling him that Grandpa has gone away only for a little while and that one day Timmy will be reunited with him. That alone will create confusion and more than likely lead to a cognitive meltdown.

I have actually gone to a hospital to visit a dying church member. As I got to the room the doctor was having a conversation with a family member. I knew that the person had just died. There was a small child clinging to the pant leg of her mother listening to the doctor. The doctor being sensitive to the small child used the phrase "expired" as opposed to died so as to shield the child from the reality of the situation. I bristled at the term "expired." To me expired is something that happens to milk after it passes the expiration date on the carton. I don't know, but somehow "expired" relates to products and shelf life, not a human being. My mind began to paint a mental picture of every person having an expiration date stamped on their forehead and that caused me anxiety. I actually ended up turning around and taking a walk to clear my head because of it before returning to the room to console the family.

Teaching someone with autism to use appropriate phrases

Knowing what is an appropriate phrase to use when acknowledging someone's death to a grieving person doesn't come naturally to someone on the autism spectrum. For that matter people in general don't know what to say when someone loses a loved one either. It creates awkwardness because no words can really bring comfort, yet people feel compelled to say something to a grieving person. Sometimes they ramble on about how wonderful the deceased person was in attempts to cheer up the grieving relative. Other times they may just say, "Sorry for your loss" because that is the most socially accepted phrase to use.

I have had numerous complaints from family and friends over inappropriate phrases used by autistic individuals in a funeral setting. Part of the problem is a lack of emphasis on teaching socially appropriate behaviors for dealing with death because it is such an unpleasant topic. This lack of emphasis is born out of the societal reluctance to deal with the whole topic of death and dying in general when there is no immediate need, preferring to deal with it only when the time comes. For instance, how many commercials have you seen on television for funeral homes that advertise the best prices in town on funeral packages? Have you ever seen a funeral home have a "year's end clearance sale" on carry over models of caskets? Of course not, because that would degrade the solemnity of the entire death experience.

This reluctance gives birth to cultural euphemisms that portray death in a less serious manner. While there is nothing inherently wrong with using those expressions in daily conversations, they become completely inappropriate in a funeral setting. For a person with autism who learns such expressions, the danger is that without proper social skills training in this area, they could use those expressions at the worst possible moments, such as when offering condolences to a grieving person. The last thing you want to hear from an autistic person at a wake who is talking to a grieving family member is "at least he's out of his misery." This is particularly a concern for autistic adults who don't have access to social skill building sessions. Because they are adults it is assumed that they would just somehow know what would be appropriate. Especially if they live independently and aren't exposed to the death and dying process. If their only exposure on how to refer to death comes from television and colloquial slang expressions, how can one expect them to know what is appropriate?

Top 20 euphemisms for death

I went on the internet to look up phrases that convey death and the list was endless. I was actually quite amazed at the creativity of the non-autistic world for coming up with some really colorful and even sort of funny (in a morbid kind of way) euphemisms. The following expressions, while common in everyday usage, aren't appropriate for use during the funeral process:

1. Buying a one-way ticket

2. Checking out

3. Croaked

4. Bought the farm

5. Dying with one's boots on

6. Horizontal mute

7. Giving up the ghost

8. On one's last leg

9. Dirt nap

10. Out of one's misery

11. Pushing up daisies

12. Biting the dust

13. Cashing in one's chips

14. Sleeping with the fishes

15. Counting worms

16. Worm buffet

17. Having one foot in the grave

18. Six feet under

19. Wearing the wooden coat

20. Deep six

Creating a conversational script

I feel the best way to "teach" someone with autism on what to say to someone who is grieving is to create a written script of what to say. Use a social story that explains the setting where potential contact with a grieving mourner may take place. Be sure to explain that colloquial expressions and euphemisms aren't appropriate because they don't convey a sense of sympathy for such a serious occasion. Write down on a piece of paper what appropriate expressions are to be used. Explain that at times like these, sometimes saying very little is better than rambling on no matter who else is doing so. The goal is not to try to cheer someone up who is grieving, but to show that you acknowledge the emotional pain they must be experiencing over their loss. Have the autistic individual rehearse what and how to say their condolence phrase. Spell out when it is an appropriate time for them to approach the grieving person. Role play with them.

Personally, I find the over-used trite expression, "Sorry for your loss" very sterile and near insulting when not conveyed with sincerity. It seems almost an obligatory response when you mention to someone that you have lost someone through death. When it is said just to fulfill societal expectations of acknowledgment, it becomes meaningless. To be truthful I find that there are no "good" expressions that can ease someone's grief during this time.

Speaking through actions

My suggestion is to say very little, if anything at all, and instead convey your sympathy through actions. People with autism tend not to be very demonstrative in showing affection. Yes we will come and want hugs when we have a need, but to volunteer a hug without being asked to for someone else who needs one is uncommon. How we tend to show "affection" is not through flowery words but through actions. I am not very emotionally demonstrative with my "love" for my husband. I do not like public displays of affection. Still whenever I travel somewhere, I make it a point to go out of my way to buy him some specialty ales to drink. His hobby is enjoying different ales from all over the world. We live in a rural part of Maine where there isn't any emphasis on fancy ales. To him such a "kind gesture" proves my love to him. I demonstrate my caring for him through various actions that show that I have thought about him when we were apart. Numerous parents have also shared with me how their autistic son or daughter has done similar actions to convey their affection.

Encourage the person with autism to convey their sympathy through hugs (if they can tolerate that), cards, getting the mourner something to eat or drink, or any practical thing they can do to help at that time. Have them say very little if anything at all. Use expressions that are truthful and sincere such as "I am so sorry" or "I will be praying for you" (if the person with autism is actually going to do that). Sometimes just sitting quietly in the background sends a silent message of support to the bereaved person.

When I attend funerals I always make it a point to extend a hug of condolence and volunteer to help with anything practical that needs to be done at the time or later on. Since I have become a well-known figure in the autism world, there is this tendency at any gathering for people to want to focus their attention on me. As a social setting rule I created for myself regarding wakes, funerals, and memorial services, I do not engage in talking about myself during such a gathering. I explain politely that I am here to offer my condolences and that I do not wish to detract attention away from the bereaved person. I then give out my business card and tell them they can contact me at a later time. I go on to explain that I am not trying to be unsocial, but that this is my "rule" regarding such an event. Because I explain myself, people understand where I am coming from and do not get offended.

Speaking through actions rather than words comes more natural for many on the spectrum. Performing some random act of kindness such as getting a plate of food for the mourner or helping serve food to the funeral party not only serves as a kind gesture, but also gives the autistic person a script to get through the event. Sometimes just sitting around quietly is too demanding for someone with autism. Perhaps it might be best for that person to do something actively by offering assistance rather than forcing them to stay seated to endure the gathering. Channel their nervous energy from sitting and stimming into serving others. Staying busy with some task is a great compromise for involving someone with autism in the funeral proceedings who otherwise couldn't sit through the entire function.

There is always this sense of helplessness felt by all those who attend such a function: helplessness in the sense of not being able to say or do anything to ease the pain of the people who are mourning. Participating in some physical aspect allows one to feel like they are doing something and thereby not feel so helpless. Volunteering to serve at such gatherings not only helps ease the anxiety of the autistic individual but also will be seen in a favorable light by others.

CHAPTER 5

How to Tell a Person with Autism Someone Died

I feel it is prudent to have a plan of action in place before having to break the news to an autistic person that someone they know has died. Ideally, if possible include the autistic individual in drawing up this action plan. This way it begins a dialogue for discussing what to expect when the time comes. It allows the individual to contribute what would be helpful as well as open them up to the absoluteness of death. It will also alert you to potential areas of anxiety that may occur once the news is given, especially if during the formation of this plan the ASD individual begins to show anxiety just by talking about a particular issue or concern. I know that it is an unpleasant subject even to consider but force yourself to deal with it before a death occurs. Since people with autism hate surprises, having a pre-planned script of what to do and expect will greatly aid in managing the difficulties that such a transition will impart.

If you are a parent of adult children on the spectrum, face the reality that your son or daughter one day will more than likely have to live through your or your spouse's death. When you are no longer there to care and comfort them through such ordeals, how will they manage the funeral process? What about the ASD individual deeply attached to a grandparent, or elderly relative or friend? Do you know what to do when they spiral into a meltdown over the news? When an unexpected sudden death occurs, how prepared are you in breaking that news to someone with autism? What is your plan for the fallout once the news is broken? If the death affects you personally (having to make funeral arrangements or feeling devastated by the loss), will you be able to give 100 percent of your attention to this plan?

Recently while visiting my dear friend Cathy, we discussed this very issue. Besides having a non-verbal young adult son on the spectrum, she works for the autism society in our state. Because of her work she also knew my friend and colleague Will. I wish we had prepared a plan of what to do at the time of Will's illness but we didn't. It was through trial and error of what to do next during that period that this action plan was born. She witnessed how difficult this transition was for me. Only through her patience and understanding did I come to realize two years after Will's death how important it is to have someone who can guide us through such a painful ordeal. At the end of this chapter you will find a template for an action plan. It is merely a generic guide. Feel free to modify it to fit the needs of the person it is being drawn up for. I cannot stress enough how important it is to create a separate form for each ASD individual which addresses their specific concerns and needs.

Establishing a "point person"

Once the form is finished, it is imperative to establish a point person that knows about this document and how to handle the needs of the autistic individual. A point person is someone who will be able to detach emotionally from the deceased person. Sometimes it will be a non-family member or friend who isn't directly impacted by the death. Or it could be a family member who won't be distracted by all the procedures required in arranging a funeral. It is the person who will inform the autistic individual about someone's death and also act as a guide helping them through the funeral process. This is a person familiar with the autistic individual's strengths, limitations, and triggers. It is someone who the ASD individual is familiar with, trusts, and is comfortable around especially when they are anxious. I have people that I am familiar with and trust but would not want around when I am deeply distressed, especially if it revolves around a death. No offense to them but I know they would be uncomfortable and unable to handle me should I spiral downwards into a meltdown. Be in agreement of who the point person will be *with* the autistic individual before the need arises.

Death leaves us all feeling vulnerable and emotions are raw and sometimes unrestrained. Things may be said by autistic individuals about the deceased person they don't really mean, such as "They are better off dead" or

"I'm glad they are gone." This is pure wounded emotion and an expression of emotional pain that needs to be vented. If the person in charge of this plan is emotionally involved with the deceased person, they may respond back negatively, creating a conflict needlessly. The person in charge must understand that these comments are benign and just an emotional expression of grief and not react to them at all.

This point person will also recognize that many ASD individuals have issues and fears of abandonment. Death is the ultimate in being abandoned. It might take a lot of reassurances and feel like a broken record, but it is vital in combating the intense fears surrounding unpredictability that death creates.

The point person may also be the one who deals with the aftermath of a loss of housing as a result of the death. This would be the case if the ASD individual is living with someone who dies and can't function alone in that environment. Assistance will be required in helping them find new living arrangements. Again the exact role of the person in charge will depend on the needs of the autistic individual. It is important to determine in advance just how much responsibility will be necessitated.

Notifying the ASD individual someone has died

Notifying the person is the actual breaking of the news. Does the individual want to be informed of someone's death in person, over the phone, by postal mail, or by email? How to notify someone will depend on their preference as well as their coping skills for dealing with such news. For some people on the autism spectrum, being told over the phone will completely blindside them and possibly send them spiraling into a meltdown. This wouldn't be a good scenario if they received the news when they are alone or are engaged in some activity in public, where if they spiral there is a danger to their safety. For others, being notified by email or regular mail allows them the alone time to process the news without having to engage in interactions and conversations which could become cognitively overwhelming to them at that moment.

Be very mindful of where the news is given. Wait until you have them in a setting where they will be able to self-soothe and react in a way that won't disrupt others around them. It wouldn't be a good idea to just pull them out of the classroom or work environment for a few minutes to deliver such shocking news and then expect them after a brief respite to resume their day. Don't interrupt an important routine or activity just to tell them either. The person who died isn't going anywhere anytime soon so wait until the end of the day or when things are quiet to inform them of someone's death.

Personally, I prefer being told in person. The shock of such news tends to incapacitate me initially. Having someone there to help redirect my thoughts and offer practical suggestions that help with re-establishing a working routine throughout the entire process from death to burial is invaluable to me. With my history of impulsivity and a definite lack in executive functioning skills, being left unattended after such news allows for poor judgment. What I may think is a great idea at the time may actually be unwise or unsafe. One of my most useful calming strategies is that I like to walk out my anxiety. While there is nothing inherently wrong with that strategy, the problem lies in differentiating when I shouldn't implement it. As I write this chapter it is January and here in northern Maine it is -18 degrees Fahrenheit outside today with a wind-chill factor of -35 degrees Fahrenheit. Exposed skin will freeze after only ten minutes of exposure. If I were to receive such distressing news today, I would automatically commence going for a walk. The shock of the news would paralyze my ability of discerning whether it would be safe or not to venture outside. If someone is with me as the news is broken, they would be able to redirect my attention onto a calming strategy that wouldn't cause imminent danger to my safety.

Knowing what to expect after the ASD individual finds out the person died

It would be most helpful if the autistic individual could themselves describe how they would react and behave under such a circumstance before it occurs. Be prepared for a whole myriad of emotional outbursts and actions that may seem inappropriate for the circumstance. Be prepared for very blunt questions surrounding the death and regarding interruptions in their routines. If the death was unexpected and very sudden, particularly if it involves someone young, there is a chance that the autistic person may fear that the same thing will happen to them. Sudden unforeseen deaths are illogical in the natural cycle of life and death in general. If the death was the result of a car accident, that individual may fear going any place in a vehicle because of the unpredictability and randomness of who ends up "chosen" to die in a crash. Remember to use facts and not reassuring phrases such as "Don't worry, you'll be fine" when helping with alleviating such a fear. Use statistics and facts that demonstrate the safety of traveling by automobiles.

This is the time when people involved with the autistic individual should know what would be helpful for that person such as them being left alone or needing a hug. Have the autistic individual create a list of things that would be helpful for others to do for them and what they should expect in the event of a death. If the person with autism is incapable of doing so, have the point person explain to those who will have contact with the individual how to react and what to say or not say.

Now will be the time to discuss whether or not the individual can or can't participate in the wake or ceremony. If they want to participate then work on a script. If they feel they absolutely can't, then respect and convey that decision to the parties involved. Explain to the funeral party that it is autism and not an indifference to the deceased person or mourners that prevents their attendance.

Setting up plans (scripts) and contingencies to be utilized from death through interment

Basically this is a script for getting through the entire process from receiving the news right through to the burial or cremation. I am a big proponent of at least one backup script or plan because many meltdowns are the result of a deviation from an established script.

Death can be a very chaotic time for the bereaved person. Simple things may become overlooked during the emotional turmoil that is experienced by those left behind. Having a detailed written script of how the day will unfold will greatly help the person with autism cope with all the spontaneous changes the day may hold as the result of a death. Since normal routines will more than likely be suspended, having a written plan to follow will aid in restoring a sense of order to the autistic individual during such times of great upheaval to their normal daily structure.

Try to create alternate backup plans or scripts just in case the intended script or plan needs to be altered due to some unforeseen circumstance such as inclement weather delaying the burial, or holding off on the ceremony due to late arrivals. Sometimes spur of the moment unplanned decisions to go out for dinner can create great distress in the autistic individual.

Also have an "escape plan" as a backup scripted out. This is what I would refer to as an emergency "bail out" procedure; what to do if for some reason anywhere during the proceedings or gatherings the autistic individual becomes overly stressed and needs to leave. Write it up as a written plan which can be followed in the arranged sequence by either the autistic person or point person so as to cause minimal disruption to others at the ceremony or gathering afterward.

Setting up plans for two alternate scenarios

It is really prudent to have a plan for what to do for both expected and unexpected deaths. One plan would be to handle a foreseeable death such as a terminal illness or advanced old age. The other plan would be for unanticipated death like accidents, or sudden death from a congenital abnormality for instance. Each plan would be unique in its approach to guide and assist the autistic individual through the transition of death and the changes that will occur as a result.

Particularly for terminal illnesses it is important to prepare ahead of time for the certainty of that person dying. This is the time to slowly start to modify the routines that will be impacted by that person's death. In my case with Will, there were so many times I couldn't visit him in the hospital because the chemotherapy depleted his immune system and he was placed in isolation. We would talk to each other over the phone instead. I wasn't fond of that idea but there was no alternative to maintaining contact. In hindsight, I now recognize that while at the time I was resistant to this "change" in our routine, it was a routine that became modified for my own good. Slowly through this process I began to accept that I couldn't see him and in the end that "modification" made it easier to transition towards never being able to see him again.

What I am about to say next may come across as controversial and cold hearted, but in my experience I feel cutting some of the ties to the person who is dying will help avoid the blindside of their death. I am not advocating a total rejection of the dying person. My concern is as it was for me, that I became very dependent on Will. He was very important to me as a friend and adoptive parental figure. We saw each other weekly and spoke over the phone daily. I couldn't imagine life without him. Those that knew me feared that I would handle his death poorly. I used to get extremely upset whenever I even thought of him dying before he was diagnosed with leukemia.

His leukemia forced us to cut some of the ties between us. Not only couldn't we see each other as we had, but also his priorities shifted to family business and concerns. There wasn't much one on one quality time any more for us. While that was still very difficult to accept, I knew on a subconscious level that this was a major part of the transition I would have to endure when he died. This "separation" while he was still alive helped tremendously with my having to design new routines to take the place of all the routines I had developed that included him. All my protesting couldn't alter these changes to our routine. I had no choice but to deal with it.

I really want to qualify what I just said. This will be a very personal decision and must be decided on an individual case-by-case basis. Part of human nature surrounding terminal illness begs for as much time with the dying person as possible. I understand that completely. I worry about the autistic child who is so overly attached to the dying person who without some transition separation becomes unable to accept the reality of death when it occurs. This holds true for a grandparent whose health is in decline. Now would be the best time to acclimatize the ASD individual that death will be imminent. Explain to the child or adult what is happening in as much detail as they can handle and request. It would also be a good time to create and begin to implement replacement routines that will take over for the ones lost with the death of the person.

Nothing will ever replace the person who dies and we autistics know that too. But when someone becomes the center of our focus for so long that we create extra meaningful routines that encompass them, then our world centers around that individual. Those routines with that person bring predictability and stability. Losing that significant person from our life throws our entire world into instability and unpredictability. We will tend to focus on fixing the problem when they die and with death there is no "fix" so we must strive to create a new reality that will restore our sense of stability and predictability. I am only offering up a practical strategy from a logical standpoint. It may benefit only a small percentage of the autistic population out there; you must decide if this is even a viable option for the autistic individual in your life.

I speak from the autistic vantage point. Having to lose someone so dear to me was beyond traumatic. I explained to Will that I couldn't be at his side when he died after his remission ended. I explained that I couldn't give concrete reasons as to why I didn't want to see him decline in the last weeks of his life. He knew why and told me that he understood and gave me permission to keep my distance. Although he missed me, he was wise enough to comprehend that I would struggle tremendously with his death. He felt that this "distance" would be beneficial in my transition of losing him and he actually encouraged it. That was a true sign of altruistic love; to put my needs above his.

Understanding why an autistic person refuses further contact with those associated with the deceased person

It is important for you to understand that autistic people approach friendship much differently than non-autistic people do. For instance, I had a very close friendship with Will. On rare occasions Will's wife would join in on one of our activities. I didn't mind that as I enjoyed conversing with her when the opportunity arose. Only on very rare occasions did the three of us do anything together. Apart from that, my time and focus was on my friend Will. When he died I broke off all contact with his family including his wife. I did this not to be cruel and heartless, but in my autistic mind I wasn't "friends" with his wife so there was no connection to her after his death. The same has occurred with my stepsister. After my stepfather died, she and I completely lost contact. She didn't live with us and I saw her very infrequently when my stepfather was alive. Again in my mind I felt no connection to her as she didn't live with us and was only connected to me through a marriage which terminated upon his death.

The friend of my friend isn't automatically my "friend." They may be an acquaintance but not a friend, unless I cultivate a one on one relationship with that acquaintance. For many people with autism this mindset holds true. Once the significant person is out of the picture, all their (the person who left or died) contacts are too unless we have established a personal relationship with them. A personal relationship means more than acknowledging they exist; it means that we have had contact enough that we developed a routine that incorporates that individual as an inner circle friend. For instance I am close friends with Cathy. When I spend the night at her house (she lives a four-hour drive away) I spend time talking to her husband about mutual topics of interest while I wait for her when she is busy. I enjoy these talks with him because we have a special interest in common. The point is that Cathy is my main friend. Our time frame together is mainly a one on one. Her husband is just someone I converse with because he is present in the period when she is busy. When he isn't present, he doesn't even register in my brain. Should Cathy die, I would not seek further contact with her husband because I was friends with Cathy and not him (technically).

Don't be offended if the autistic individual in your life does the same thing after someone they were close to dies. It is not an act of antisocial behavior as it is a reflection of their mindset regarding friendships and relationships. Not wanting to maintain contact with long lost relatives who want to pursue further contact with the ASD individual is normal. If they didn't have an existing relationship before the funeral, it will be impossible to expect them to just embrace something that is unfamiliar to them.

Coping with the death of a pet

To many people pets are a very important part of their lives. While I have a farm full of barnyard pets, my house cats are an extremely important facet of my life. They bring joy and comfort and I couldn't imagine life without them. I have lost numerous cats over the course of my life and their death was always very difficult to get through. I tried to accept the bio-cycle of life approach that deals with understanding life expectancies of different animals. This is a concept promoted in some autism circles as a way to desensitize, teach, and prepare an ASD individual for the death of pets and humans. Knowing in advance that cats only live to be around 15 years old doesn't make losing that cat any easier.

I have found that the emptiness and void of that beloved animal left behind in the house is too profound for me. I have chosen a logical practical solution in dealing with losing one of my beloved pet house cats. I have multiple cats at one time. I have staggered their ages so that they don't all die around the same time. It actually helps me embrace the cycle of life and death better. I have a cat now that I am very fond of who is 15 years old. She is becoming thin and prefers to sleep most of the time. I also have two young kittens that spend their days getting into countless mischief. Their youthful antics always bring joy to my heart. It also offsets the void that will be created by my older cat in the near future. I have adopted the reasoning that the death of one animal allows an opening for another. Since *all* my cats are rescue cats that were doomed for euthanasia, I choose to view the passing of one of my cats as a way to save the life of another. It doesn't take away the sorrow I feel but it does help to know that there is some good that can come out of death.

For those of you who have only one pet at a time I strongly advocate "replacement therapy." By that I mean introducing a younger version of the pet while the original one is still alive so as to ease the transition of losing the older one. It allows the person with autism to slowly transition their focus onto the younger pet and create new routines while still having the older pet around. There is nothing worse than having a pet die and then waiting to find a new pet. That wait period where the routines are abruptly broken will be extremely traumatic for someone on the spectrum. Again this is just a thought to consider. I have utilized this "replacement" technique on myself for the last 26 years and it has helped me tremendously in accepting the death of my pets.

The template form

I am going to put this generic form in the first person from the autistic point of view. Because this form should be discussed with the ASD individual I feel it is best if we (autistics) whenever possible advocate for ourselves what it is we need. This way there is a minimal chance of miscommunication of our needs. This form is just a rough guide but will give you an idea of what things to be mindful of. Modify this form to suit the needs of the person it is drawn up for.

HOW TO TELL YOU SOMEONE DIED

- By phone.

- In person.

- By postal mail.

- By email.

WHAT TO EXPECT AFTER YOU FIND
OUT THE PERSON DIED

- My initial reaction and what behaviors I might manifest.

- What people can do that would be helpful for me, for example, leave me alone, check in on me, stay with me.

- Why I can or can't participate in the wake, ceremony, funeral, or gathering.

SETTING UP A PLAN (SCRIPT) FOR GETTING THROUGH THE FUNERAL PROCESS

- Familiarize yourself with the location and the venue.

- Ensure you have a detailed itinerary of what will occur during the ceremony, including a timeline of events.

- Discuss appropriate behaviors and prepare stim tools to control your stress levels.

HAVING ONE PLAN FOR EXPECTED DEATHS (TERMINAL ILLNESS, ADVANCED OLD AGE)

- Write out a daily script of what to do and when.

- Rehearse my script of how to interact with others during proceedings and gatherings.

- Have alternate scripts just in case there are deviations in the planned activities.

HAVING A SEPARATE PLAN FOR UNEXPECTED DEATHS (FATAL ACCIDENTS)

- Write out a daily script of what to do and when.

- Rehearse my script of how to interact with others during proceedings and gatherings.

- Have alternate scripts just in case there are deviations in the planned activities.

CREATING AN EXIT PLAN IN CASE I GET TOO STRESSED

- Recognize warning signs that I am getting anxious.

- Have a signal that I can use with someone to alert them I need to leave.

- Seat myself within the ceremony or gathering so it is easier to leave without being disruptive to others.

- Have self-soothing strategies or stim tool at hand that I can use discreetly in front of others in case I feel my anxiety level rising.

ON REFLECTION

In conclusion I want to note that I have excluded any real reference to faith and religion. Religion if it is practiced is an integral part of the death and dying process. Having a belief system of any sort will greatly aid in comforting the mourners by giving them hope that they will one day be reunited with their loved one in another realm or existence. For the purpose of this book, however, I have kept the focus mainly on the practical side of addressing death and grief from a merely logical autistic point of view as opposed to from a theological point of view. For the autistic individual with a religious belief system, please incorporate your beliefs into the strategies outlined within this book.

Death is a very personal issue and no one person's experience, theory, or book on the matter defines how *every* autistic person will experience grief and loss. I used my personal examples to give you some idea of what it was like for me as an autistic individual. I have spoken with quite a few autistic teens and adults over this very issue of death. Much of my book reflects the general consensus I found among those I interviewed, but it is still just a book meant as a guide and does not reflect how every person on the spectrum feels and reacts to this topic.

CHAPTER 6

Death as a Special Interest

One of the most frequently asked questions I receive centers on why autistic children and teens seem drawn to making death their special interest. Frankly it seems to scare a lot of people because it is unnatural to make "death" a hobby. The societal assumption is that the only people who "obsess" over death are sociopaths and serial killers. True, there are a large number of children and adults with autism who focus on death as their special interest, but not because of some mental derangement. Autistic people have an innate need for facts and a quest for answers to unanswerable questions. In order for us to fully comprehend a subject of interest, we study it in depth. Believe it or not, special interests are a major coping strategy in dealing with our emotions. Special interests allow us to feel elation and combat sadness. It is a vent for our repressed emotions. Individuals who have death as their special interest have it for some specific reason.

Some reasons why an autistic individual chooses the topic of death as a special interest

A NEED TO KNOW

The main reason is for a need to know. No one really concretely knows what happens to us when we die. Those who embrace a religious faith believe (based on that faith) there is some sort of eternal reward that awaits them upon death. There is supposition and speculation about the afterlife as well as downright denial of any further existence after death. The fact that the topic of death isn't brought up as a source of everyday discussion creates a sense of curiosity in an ASD individual. That innate need to find answers to the questions of life fuels our desire to study the subject. Death is a scary topic for anyone. Some autistic individuals will study death in order to stem their fear of it. The more they gather facts, the less frightening death becomes because knowledge curbs the fear of unknowns. Schools provide health and sex education but not education on death and dying (biology notwithstanding). I know it is because schools don't want to frighten the children, which is understandable. However, without formal instruction children will pick up information on their own or through the media. Autistic teens and adults in their thirst of answers will focus on fact gathering.

At one of my lectures, a speech language pathologist came up to me for advice on how to handle a situation she felt was very disturbing. She had a social skills building group comprised of autistic middle school children aged between 11 and 14. Her intentions were to teach appropriate and correct conversational skills. The group wasn't very cooperative and moments of awkward silence dominated the hour-long sessions. In attempts to raise interest, the speech language pathologist decided to use special interests as a catalyst to start the conversation among the group.

She pointed to one young man and asked him to explain for five minutes to the group what his special interest was. He blurted out that his special interest was ancient Egyptian mummification practices and rattled off a bunch of facts in regards to the subject. The other autistic members of this group became so fascinated with the topic that their attention was riveted on this young man's explanations. They began asking questions, which soon led to conversations about other aspects of death. The entire group became so animated and excited over talking about death that she was unable to redirect them to an entirely different topic. The young man's interest in this rather bizarre topic began after he watched the latest Hollywood movie version of *The Mummy*. The movie actually went into detail on the process of the mummification of a "cursed" live person. He began his special interest to validate the authenticity of such an event actually happening.

To me it was quite obvious that the entire group shared a similar curiosity about death. Finally they were given a chance to explore this topic publicly. The conversations centered on factual exchanges and not on the prospects of carrying out such a practice on someone today. There were no latent desires to harm another human being. The excitement displayed over this subject is what frightened the speech language pathologist. She wanted to know from me if she should be concerned for her personal safety as a result of this. Once I explained to her why this topic was so electrifying to the group, it laid her fears to rest. That circumstance became the catalyst for a very successful social skills building class on exploring death and dying in a controlled and appropriate manner.

A SENSE OF CLOSURE

Another major reason for a special interest in death, particularly if it begins after the loss of someone the autistic individual was familiar with, is for a sense of closure. Let's face it, death brings out intense feelings of helplessness to those who have to witness its progression. We are powerless to stop it and are forced to sit by and do nothing when death comes to claim someone we know. Death in its wake leaves many unanswered questions. The autistic mindset which focuses on its elusive search for concrete answers to every question will channel that helplessness into studying about death. They no longer feel helpless because in their mind they are taking action by studying the subject that left them powerless. I know this may seem foreign but there is this sense of closure and victory in understanding how death works. Particularly with mass shootings and the media hype surrounding the incident, there is a sense of powerlessness felt even by society as a whole, as all we can do is watch the tragedy unfold on our television sets.

My mother witnessed the horrors of war as a child in Europe during the Second World War. As a young child I remember her recounting stories of losing family members in horrific ways, as well as the destruction and terror that advancing armies brought with them. I had aunts, uncles, and cousins I would never meet because they died in the war. Many of them lie in unmarked mass graves. Hearing those stories brought on a sense of helplessness and an inability to find closure within me. By the time I was six years old and in grade school I had a deep interest in the European theater during the war. I didn't focus on the battles per se, but the wake of death left in their aftermath. I was particularly fascinated with war atrocities against civilians, especially the Holocaust.

My mother was traumatized by the atrocities she was forced to watch as a child. I felt helpless when she had periods where she would cry over tragic childhood memories. In my autistic brain it brought closure for me to study and thereby understand what death must have looked like to her. It was my autistic way of expressing to her that "I understand what you must have gone through." My mother was very distressed at this special interest of mine and I know it brought her a lot of sadness. The more I collected facts and military artifacts, the more excited I became because there was this sense of taking back control and not feeling so helpless. Unfortunately my enthusiasm was misinterpreted as a disturbed obsession with the macabre. It was a sense of tension between us all throughout my growing up. It was a special interest that could not be denied. This special interest also didn't help my popularity with my fellow classmates and teachers. To them little girls should be obsessed with dolls and not war atrocities. I was regarded by my classmates as a "weirdo-freak."

My military collecting career began in grade school and continues today. I have a very large collection of combat militaria including thousands of original graphic combat photographs. I also have a collection of original photographs from the Holocaust, atomic bombings of Nagasaki and Hiroshima, as well as civilian atrocities in the Pacific. These photographs to me bring a sense of closure. It is my way of understanding visually the atrocity that befell them. I handle these photos with respect and honor. They aren't something I am excited to show others. Matter of fact, they are so private I don't share them with anyone including my husband. To some non-autistic individuals this "hobby" of mine appears grossly abnormal because what kind of person even wants to be reminded of such horrors. To me it helps with my understanding that we are all going to die someday and not all by old age either. Photographic reminders of war deaths bring forth the realization that no matter what country one lives in, war knows no boundaries. It has actually made me more of an activist for world peace. By becoming more of an activist, it has aided in closure regarding all my relatives who died in such unspeakable war atrocities.

RISING TELEVISION POPULARITY OF THE PARANORMAL

In recent years there has been an explosion of reality television programs on ghost hunting. This has spawned a cultural interest in the paranormal among young adults. I have investigated the paranormal ever since I was a young teen and now I have founded my own paranormal investigation group. I really developed that as a special interest at a young age due in part to the news that my stepfather was going to die from cancer. I needed concrete proof that there was an afterlife. Stories of ghosts had always intrigued me so I set out to prove their existence. Now I have all the sophisticated and high tech tools in the field to do this. For me it isn't a "hobby" but a scientific research project looking to record on electronic media the continuity of life. I have managed to capture some irrefutable evidence that to me documents the validity of life after death. My secondary "special interest" is in the demonic and helping people oppressed by such forces within their home. It has become a lifelong vocation which I pursue not for "fun" but for altruistic reasons.

For some people with autism, such television shows has sparked a thirst for knowledge regarding the supernatural. I have had more and more autistic teens and adults share with me that they too are deeply interested in paranormal research. "Ghost hunting" (a term I actually find disrespectful to the dead and somewhat offensive) is a hobby comprised of gathering data via scientific instruments. Evidence captioned on electronic media provides concrete evidence of some sort of existence after death. It is also very popular with teens today and for an autistic teen looking for a place to fit in with his or her peers, this provides an avenue for that. I would be remiss if I didn't warn you that paranormal investigation can be harmful. Apart from the obvious dangers of wandering around at night in unfamiliar places in the pitch dark, dealing with the spirit world can be very dangerous. It is a field of study that should be respected and not seen as an opportunity for thrill seekers.

ZOMBIE AND VAMPIRE MANIA

Ever since the release of a series of movies chronicling the saga of two young teen vampires in love, there has been this widespread fascination with the undead. Hit movies about zombies invading our world have also contributed to this popularity of the horror genre in society. I have seen all sorts of merchandise including a slew of books on how to survive a zombie attack. Apparently killing zombies is an art form well detailed in these books as well as in television and in the movies. Teenagers, whether they are autistic or not, are captivated by this craze embracing the "undead" as their special interest.

I had a consultation regarding a young autistic teen and his "obsessive" special interest on edged weaponry such as swords, hatchets, and the like. He specialized in the composition of the metal for the blades and which metal was most suitable for beheading a person with just one blow. The school became extremely worried because this young man would draw edged weapons and then proudly show them to his classmates, complete with a description of how much human strength would be required to deliver a single fatal blow to a person's head.

Upon talking with the young man I discovered his "special interest" came about from watching an apocalyptic television series based on zombies killing off and eating alive all humankind. The plot was so plausible that this young man became very convinced of the reality of such an event. He decided to read up on how to protect himself from a zombie attack and found out the only way to kill a zombie was to destroy its brain, preferably by shooting it in the head or beheading. Knowing he was too young to own a gun, he concentrated on edged weapons. This developed into a special interest as he explored what weaponry would be best suitable for self-protection. He got caught up in the manufacturing process of edged weapons of swords and daggers and focused mainly on that aspect. The more he immersed himself in that study, the more his connection to zombies faded. Eventually it wasn't obvious even to him why he focused on swords and beheadings. This is why initially his interest came across as alarming and dangerous to the safety of the other students. Not knowing where that interest stemmed from painted a picture of a very disturbed young man plotting a killing spree.

As in the case with this young man, so much of television and the movies contain graphic detailed scenes of violence and death which can frighten impressionable minds. The autistic approach is centered on problem solving. It is common for an autistic individual to read up on facts on any facet of what they saw on television to either prove or disprove its validity. The problem comes in with our tendency to hyper-focus on some micro-element of what initially peaked our interest. For instance in the case of the young man I just mentioned, we can see that his concern and curiosity about how to kill a zombie became derailed as he explored the weaponry required for such a task. He got so caught up in the manufacturing of the weapons that it became his focal point of interest.

LOOKING TO FIT IN

Sometimes autistic children and teens pick up an obsessive interest with death because it is the special interest of the peers around him. For those autistic individuals who want to fit in with peers, they may resort to picking up such an interest just to be included. With the rise of the Goth movement, a morbid fascination with death is a requirement. Teens and adults usually dress in black with numerous references of the macabre painted, tattooed, or worn as jewelry on their body. There is this fixation with death and some parts of this subculture really lean towards the bizarre. I have seen Goth individuals with piercings all over their body and their bodies mutilated to imitate ancient African tribal customs. For some autistic teens, joining this movement is about being accepted without judgment. They find a place where they feel they belong.

FEAR

Sometimes fear can trigger a special interest in death. If an autistic child is bullied and they are threatened with such phrases as "I am going to kill you" or "You're going to die freak" by another schoolmate, this can launch a special interest in death. The autistic child may start out by searching to gather information on statistics of deaths by bullying, or how many individuals under a certain age die each year. Remember that for people with autism, there is this intense need to gather facts about a subject in order to gain an overall understanding of it. In order to stem the emotion of fear, gaining facts not only provides a logical basis for whether those fears are founded or unfounded, but also provides emotional release. There is always a great sense of pleasure that is derived from engaging in a special interest. Studying that which causes them fear is a coping strategy designed to prove or disprove the validity of such an event occurring to them.

Another avenue for fear is the violence on television and in the media. Not a day goes by where we don't hear about a murder, suicide, or fatal accident close to home. The news media focuses more on bad news than good news. Shocking tragedies are always front and center while stories of goodwill receive minimal attention. We are bombarded by such tragedies on the nightly news casts. The world is portrayed as a dangerous place to live.

Schools in the United States are now locked down while in session, with many schools having armed guards watching the entrances. Metal detectors as well as a complete ban on anything that could be used as a weapon are the new "norm" for children attending public schools today. Having to attend school under these conditions can be very frightening for some children. For an autistic child or teen the uncertainty of their safety in school could be what begins their special interest in death.

NEWS OF SOMEONE'S SUDDEN DEATH

Another potential trigger for a special interest in death stems from the fear of sudden death. It is easy to explain why death occurs to someone who is old or dying of a terminal illness. Somehow that fits with the natural cycle of life. What is impossible to comprehend is sudden unexplained death whether it is from an organic cause or a mechanical one. To someone with autism the apparent "randomness" of such a death becomes very disconcerting because it is unpredictable. We hate unpredictability. There may be a fear that the same thing could happen to them. This in turn elicits an intense need to study all the facts regarding that possibility. As I said earlier, we have this tendency to hyper-focus on a very narrow part of the "whole." That means that although the special interest was launched in response to a fear of dying suddenly, they became sidetracked from some interesting component during their initial search, so that became their focal point. For instance while seeking out facts on drunk driving fatalities, they become intrigued with the statistics regarding the yearly death rate of people in various countries.

In conclusion

In conclusion I want you to understand that I don't have all the answers to the "whys" of things we autistic people do. Having a special interest in death shouldn't be automatically seen as a symptom of some underlying desire to commit murder. Generally, but not always, special interests involving death are the result of some sort of trigger. What that trigger is can be elusive and difficult to pinpoint. These interests need to be dealt with on a case-by-case basis.

Index